77 RECIPES

GUNDEL

NEW HUNGARIAN COOKBOOK

77 RECIPES

GUNDEL

NEW HUNGARIAN COOKBOOK

GUNDEL

NEW HUNGARIAN
COOKBOOK

To Laurel –
You can use this &
think of great times
in Budapest!
Love, Leigh
12/06

EXCERPTS
FROM GUNDEL'S GUESTBOOK

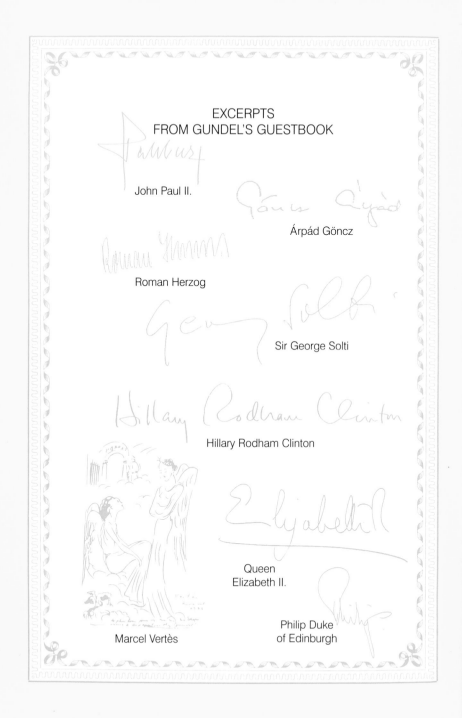

John Paul II.

Árpád Göncz

Roman Herzog

Sir George Solti

Hillary Rodham Clinton

Queen
Elizabeth II.

Marcel Vertès

Philip Duke
of Edinburgh

Kálmán Kalla

NEW HUNGARIAN COOKBOOK

with Zoltán Halász

Introduction by George Lang

Photos by
LÁSZLÓ CSIGÓ

Designed by
FERENC SKOLLÁR

Copy Editor
MARY GOODBODY

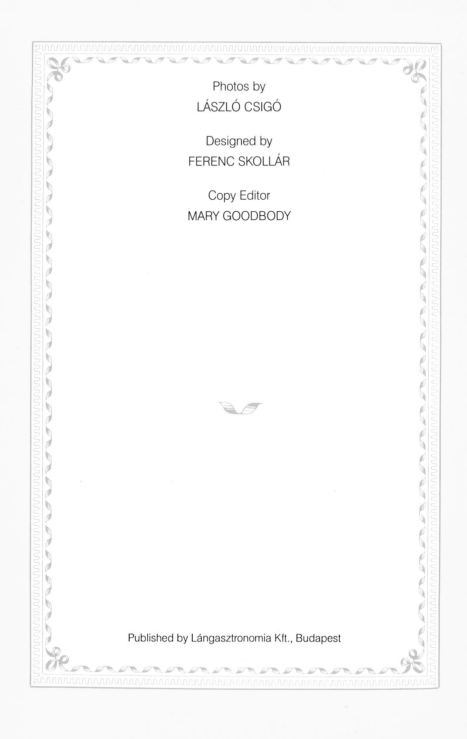

Published by Lángasztronomia Kft., Budapest

Content

A Passionate Introduction

by

GEORGE LANG

I can hear some of you asking, "Do we need another cookbook? And furthermore, do we need another Gundel cookbook?!"

After due deliberation, master chef Kálmán Kalla of Gundel, his team, Zoltán Halász, the noted historian and gastronome, and I decided that we must write and publish a new Gundel cookbook. Here are a few of our reasons:

Every restaurant gets the kind of cookbook it deserves and we all felt that we should collaborate on a book that would present some of the dishes that make the new, resurrected Gundel so beloved.

We tried to sort out great Hungarian specialties of the past and combine them with the best of the present, as defined by the joint efforts of our team during the last six years of culinary renovation. We also had the courage to eliminate certain dishes that had become more popular than they had a right to be.

Károly Gundel and his chefs created specialties that became important parts of the pre-World War II repertoire of Hungarian restaurants, but the new generation is looking for updated culinary fantasies, and foods that connect the head and the stomach.

A cookbook that is intended both for cooking and for reading should not be just a collection of fascinating sounding

but rather vague recipes, but a clearly written, user-friendly guide that eliminates the pitfalls for the person who is attempting to reproduce the food. A good cookbook should not presume that the cook has tasted the dish before, nor should it require the skill of a professional *saucier.*

I have always felt that a cookbook based on imprecise recipes is a fool's bible. There are only a handful of chefs whose recipes you can trust and even fewer whose recipes you can enjoy. Toque d'Or Chef Kalla is known for being able to write pharamaceutically-precise recipes that are innovative, informative and indispensable, with uncompromising attention to details.

The happy news is that you do not have to visit Gundel Restaurant to taste these dishes (lately, many have been served to kings, queens as well as to people who simply love good food). You can prepare them from this cookbook. This–we felt–was a good enough reason to postpone a moratorium on the publication of new cookbooks.

I am convinced that if old man Gundel came back to us after reading these recipes, he would tuck in his napkin in anticipation and enjoy the happy fact that there is life after re-birth, especially after the re-birth of the Hungarian kitchen.

I would like to raise a glas of wine (naturally from the Lauder-Lang Vineyards) in memory of those who created Gundel's magical past and to our all-star Gundel team that is creating the present and the future.

General Notes from the Chef

In some cases I have slightly altered the classic Gundel recipes for the book, conserving their original character but, in deference to the times in which we live, lightening many of them and omitting or changing certain methods, such as steaming meats and vegetables.

It is understood that the ingredients are always prepared after they have been washed or otherwise cleaned, and so we have not indicated these steps in the recipes. Likewise, we do not state that onions and garlic cloves, for example, should be peeled and cleaned before using.

When appropriate, we refer to the sauce and side dish best suited to a particular dish and have indicated where in the chapter called Sauces and Side Dishes to find this recipes. By using these accompaniments, you will achieve the best Gundel flavors.

Measures and abbreviations

1 tablespoon · a tablespoon of 15 ml volume

The word "tablespoon" in the recipes always means level (but loose, not tightly packed) spoonful, unless otherwise indicated.

1 teaspoon · a teaspoon of 5 ml volume

½ teaspoon · a teaspoon of 2 ml volume

¼ teaspoon · a teaspoon of 1 ml volume

The word "teaspoon" in the recipes always means a level (but loose, not tightly packed) spoonful, unless otherwise indicated.

1 cup · a cup of 250 ml volume

½ cup · a cup of 125 ml volume

⅓ cup · a cup of 80 ml volume

¼ cup · a cup of 60 ml volume

⅛ cup · a cup of 30 ml volume

The word "cup" in the recipes always means a level (but loose, not tightly packed) cupful, unless otherwise indicated. Dry ingredients should be measured in cups designed for dry measuring so that they can be leveled with the back of a knife or small spatula. Liquid ingredients should be measured in liquid measure cups.

Cold First Courses

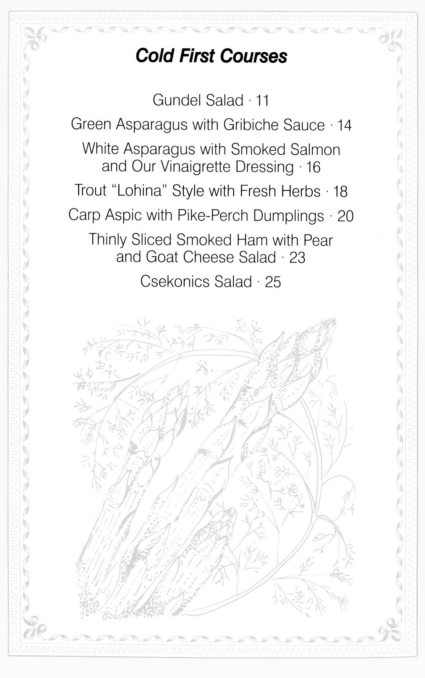

Gundel Salad · 11

Green Asparagus with Gribiche Sauce · 14

White Asparagus with Smoked Salmon
and Our Vinaigrette Dressing · 16

Trout "Lohina" Style with Fresh Herbs · 18

Carp Aspic with Pike-Perch Dumplings · 20

Thinly Sliced Smoked Ham with Pear
and Goat Cheese Salad · 23

Csekonics Salad · 25

Gundel Salad*

4 servings

1 pound mushrooms,
wiped clean with a damp paper towel,
trimmed and quartered
Salt and black pepper to taste
Juice of 1 lemon
2 tablespoons balsamic vinegar
2 tablespoons white wine vinegar
1 teaspoon confectioners' sugar
6 tablespoons olive oil
1 tablespoon Worcestershire sauce
2 tablespoons chopped fresh parsley
4 yellow bell peppers

* Gundel saláta

1 pound asparagus, preferably white asparagus
1 tablespoon granulated sugar
8 ounces green beans, trimmed
and cut into 1-inch lengths
Pinch of baking soda
4 tomatoes, 1 cucumber
2 heads Boston lettuce
12 dandelion leaves or other bitter green such
as arugula or watercress

1. Put the mushrooms in a bowl. Add salt and black pepper to taste, the lemon juice, the vinegars, the sugar, 4 tablespoons of the olive oil, the Worcestershire sauce and the parsley. Mix carefully to avoid mashing the mushrooms. Cover and refrigerate for at least 30 minutes, or longer. At the same time, put 4 salad plates in the refrigerator.

2. In a baking pan, toss the yellow peppers with the remaining 2 tablespoons of oil and put them in a pre-heated 325 °F oven. After 4 minutes, transfer to a small paper bag, seal it and set aside for 10 minutes. Peel the peppers, remove seeds and slice. Put the cooked pep-pers on a plate and sprinkle with 3 tablespoons of the liquid accumulated in the bowl holding the mushrooms.

3. Trim ½-inch from the bottom of the asparagus stems, if necessary, and if the asparagus are not young and tender, peel the stems. (See page 15. for a detailed description of how to peel asparagus). After peeling, cut into 1-inch lengths. In a large pot, bring 4 cups of water to a boil. Add the sugar and lower the heat. Add the asparagus and simmer for about 12 minutes until tender. Cool the asparagus in its cooking water for 5 minutes, and then remove from the water and set on a

plate to cool further. After 15 minutes, put the asparagus in the refrigerator for at least 30 minutes to chill.

4. In another pot, bring 4 cups of water to a boil. Add a little salt and the baking soda. Cook the green beans in the water for 3 minutes. Cool in the cooking water for 2 minutes, and then remove from the water and set on a plate to cool further. After 15 minutes, put the beans in the refrigerator for at least 30 minutes to chill.

5. Put the tomatoes in another pot of boiling water for about 1 minute until the skins crack. Remove from the boiling water and plunge into a bowl of cold water. Peel the tomatoes and cube them.

6. Halve the cucumber lengthwise, remove seeds with a spoon and slice into ¼-inch pieces. Put in a bowl, add a pinch of salt and 3 tablespoons of the liquid accumulated in the bowl holding the mushrooms.

7. Core and clean the lettuce. Tear into bite-size pieces. Wash and drain the lettuce.

8. To serve, put a pile of the torn lettuce on the chilled plates and drizzle with 2 tablespoons of the liquid accumulated in the bowl holding the mushrooms. Arrange the cooled vegetables, including the mushrooms, on the lettuce, alternating the còlors. Drizzle with the remaining mushroom liquid, dividing it equally among the plates.

I have carefully altered the famous Gundel Salad, which was created more than 50 years ago, adjusting it to modern tastes. Do not stem the mushrooms, so as to maintain their natural flavor.

Green Asparagus
with Gribiche Sauce*

4 servings

About 2 pounds green asparagus,
no more than
¼-inch in diameter
1 teaspoon salt
Pinch of baking soda
4 servings Gribiche Sauce
(see page 176.)

1. Trim ½-inch from the bottom of asparagus stems, if necessary, and if the asparagus are not young and ten-

* Hideg zöld spárga Gribiche mártással

der, peel the stems. (See below for a detailed description of how to peel asparagus.)

2. In a pot large enough to hold the asparagus on its side, bring 4 cups of the water along with the salt and baking soda to a boil. Meanwhile, put 2 cups of water and 4 or 5 ice cubes in bowl.

3. Using a slotted spoon, add the asparagus to the boiling water and cook for 1 or 2 minutes for pencil-thin asparagus and 4 or 5 minutes for slighlty thicker asparagus. Using a slotted spoon, lift the asparagus from the boiling water and immediately plunge into the ice water. Let sit for 2 minutes. Lift from the ice water, wrap in a damp kitchen towel and refrigerate for at least 20 minutes until chilled. (The asparagus can be prepared ahead of time, wrapped in plastic and refrigerated until ready to serve.)

4. Cut the asparagus into 3-inch lengths. Divide the lengths among 4 plates with the heads facing in the same direction, or arrange on a serving platter. Serve the sauce on the side.

To peel asparagus, hold the upper part of the asparagus between your thumb and index fingers and rest the lower part against your wrist to keep the vegetable from breaking when pressure is exerted with a knife. Cut into the skin 1½ inches from the head. Peel off a thin strip of the hard part. Turn the asparagus with your finger after peeling off a strip and repeat the procedure. Continue until vegetable is evenly peeled. There should be no hard outer flesh left on the asparagus.

Asparagus can also be served hot; in this case, rinse in cold water after boiling to prevent further cooking.

White Asparagus with Smoked Salmon and Our Vinaigrette Dressing*

4 servings

About 2 pounds
white asparagus,
no more than
¼-inch in diameter

1 teaspoon salt

½ teaspoon granulated sugar

8 ounces smoked salmon

1 cup Vinaigrette Dressing
(see page 176.)

** Hideg fehér spárga füstölt lazaccal
és vinaigrette mártással*

1. Trim ½-inch from the bottom of asparagus stems, if necessary, and if the asparagus are not young and tender, peel the stems. (See page 15. for a detailed description of how to peel asparagus.)

2. In a pot large enough to hold the asparagus on its side, bring 4 cups of the water along with the salt and sugar to a boil. Meanwhile, put 2 cups of water and 4 or 5 ice cubes in bowl.

3. Using a slotted spoon, add the asparagus to the boiling water and cook for 12 minutes until tender. Using a slotted spoon, lift the asparagus from the boiling water and immediately plunge into the ice water.

4. To serve, drain the asparagus, cut each stalk into 3-inch lengths and divide among the plates with the heads all facing in the same direction. Slice the smoked salmon into long ½-inch-wide strips and place alongside the asparagus. Spoon the vinaigrette sauce near the asparagus heads but do not spoon it over them.

This course is the inspiration of George Lang, who considers asparagus the queen of gastronomy. When he founded the George Lang Corporation, Milton Glaser the noted artist suggested that the subject of the logo of the new company "…should be appropriate… it must be the food you love." Lang chose a bunch of asparagus.

Trout "Lohina" Style
with Fresh Herbs[*]

4 servings

1 pound trout fillets, with skin
1 tablespoon chopped fresh parsley
Juice of ½ lemon, Salt and pepper to taste
2 tablespoons sunflower or olive oil
1 tablespoon chopped fresh dill
1 tablespoon chopped fresh sage

Potato salad
4 white or red skinned potatoes
⅓ cup white wine vinegar
2 tablespoons olive oil
3 tablespoons granulated sugar
1 tablespoon chopped fresh parsley
5½ cups water, Salt to taste
Freshly ground white pepper to taste
1 leek, trimmed and sliced into thin rings
1 head Boston lettuce for garnish
1 cup Piquant Sage Dressing (see page 178.)

1. Place the trout fillets on a plate, skin side down. Sprinkle with the lemon, parsley, salt and pepper. Take the tail end of each fillet and fold it up and over the fillets, leaving about two-thirds of the flesh exposed. Press lightly against the fold to secure it.

* Lohinai füves pisztráng

2. Heat oil in a 6-inch ovenproof frying pan and add the fish with a spatula. Bake in a preheated 325 °F oven for 15 minutes. Remove from the oil, drain on a paper towel and then let cool to room temperature.

3. Skin the fillets. Trim the fillets so that they are even and straight.

Potato Salad

1. Bring 4 cups of the water to a boil in a 2-quart pan. Boil the potatoes until tender when pierced by a fork. This should take 20 to 40 minutes, depending on the size of the potatoes. Drain and then slice the potatoes, crosswise, into ¼-inch-thick pieces using a knife with a decorative wavy edge, if possible.

2. Pour 1½ cups of water in a 2-quart bowl and add the vinegar, oil, sugar, parsley, salt and black and white pepper and stir until the sugar dissolves. Add the potatoes and leek and refrigerate for 2 to 3 hours, so that the vinegar can fully infuse the potato. (This can be prepared the night before and refrigerated until ready to serve.)

3. To serve, line each of 4 plates with 2 or 3 lettuce leaves and spoon the potato salad onto them. Place the trout fillets next to the potato salad and sprinkle with the dill and sage. Spoon a tablespoon of sage dressing near the fillets. Pass the remaining dressing.

This recipe was created by János Gundel. We served it recently as the fish course in a menu honoring the famed Hungarian writer, Mikszáth. Each dish was based on one of his favorite dishes.

Carp Aspic with Pike-Perch Dumplings*

4 appetizer servings

2 pounds fresh carp

2 pounds carp bones

1 pound red onions,
minced

1 green bell pepper,
cut into ½-inch chunks

1 tomato,
cut into ½-inch chunks

2 teaspoons sweet Hungarian paprika

Hot Hungarian paprika to taste

Salt and white pepper to taste

4 large egg whites

* Pontykocsonya fogasgaluskával

About 1½ ounces white bread dinner roll,
crusts trimmed (about half a roll),
soaked in water for 10 minutes

4 ounces fillet of pike-perch,
or any other white-fleshed fish,
such as yellow (also known as walleye) pike,
cut into ½-inch chunks

2 lemons, quartered

1. Clean and bone the carp. Put the head and bones, along with the extra carp bones in a large, heavy pot with the onions, pepper, tomato, sweet and hot paprika, salt and pepper. Cover with water and bring to a boil. Reduce heat and simmer for 1 hour. Strain liquid through a cheesecloth and set aside to cool slightly. Discard the fish bones and vegetables.

2. Whisk 2 egg whites until foamy and stir into the fish stock. Strain through cheesecloth again. Skim any impurities from the surface of the stock.

3. Squeeze out most of the water from the roll and transfer it to a food processor. Add the pike-perch, the remaining 2 egg whites and season to taste with salt and pepper. Process until ground but not completely pureed.

4. Bring 1 quart of the fish stock to a boil. Reduce heat so that the stock is simmering. Using 2 teaspoons, form the pike-perch mixture into small dumplings and drop them into the simmering stock. Cook for 5 minutes, or until dumplings are cooked through. To test, remove a dumpling from the water and cut in half. If the center is white, the fish is done. Remove the dumplings with a slotted spoon after cooking and set

aside on a plate lined with a paper towel. When cool, cover and refrigerate overnight.

5. To finish aspic, you should use small individual fish molds, or one large fish mold. Put the dumplings into the mold(s), and pour in the reserved fish stock so that it almost reaches the rim of the mold(s). Refrigerate until liquid has completely jelled, preferably overnight. Unmold onto plates or a platter, and garnish with lemon wedges and dumplings.

Thinly Sliced Smoked Ham
with Pear
and Goat Cheese Salad*

4 servings

¼ cup red bell peppers cubes
(about 1-inch-square cubes)

¼ cup green bell pepper cubes
(about 1-inch-square cubes)

¼ cup yellow bell pepper cubes
(about 1-inch-square cubes)

Salt and freshly ground
white pepper to taste

2 tablespoons olive oil

** Vékonyra szeletelt parasztsonka körtével
és juhgomolyasajt salátával*

8 ounces goat cheese,
cut into cubes

2 ounces Swiss cheese

4 medium-size ripe pears

8 ounces smoked ham,
sliced into thin pieces

1. Mix the pepper cubes with salt, pepper and olive oil. Add the goat cheese, toss gently and let rest for 30 minutes.

2. Cut the Swiss cheese into slices, about ⅛-inch thick, ½-inch wide and 2-inches long. Put 3 strips of cheese on a microwave-safe plate, arranged like a fan with the ends next to but not overlapping each other. Microwave on medium heat for 45 to 50 seconds. The cheese will melt and spread slightly on the plate.

3. Lift the cheese from the plate with a spatula and put on paper towels. After 1 or 2 minutes, it will harden and turn into a crispy, leaf-shaped cheese chip. Prepare 4 more chips with the remaining cheese.

4. Peel the pears, cut them in half and remove the cores. Cut a small piece from the curved side of each half pear so that it will lay on a plate.

5. Set 2 pear halves on each of 4 plates and fill the hollow of each with the pepper and cheese salad. Spoon any remaining salad on the plates near the pears. Place the ham slices in front of the pear. Cut a slit in the top of 1 pear half on each plate, making the cuts ¾ inch deep. Place a chip into each slot.

Csekonics Salad*

4 servings

4 boneless chicken breast halves
Salt and freshly ground white pepper to taste
1 teaspoon Hungarian sweet paprika
1 teaspoon sunflower oil
18 cooked shrimp or crayfish, shelled
4 tomatoes, 2 heads Boston lettuce
1 cup mayonnaise
Salt and cayenne pepper to taste
1 teaspoon fresh tarragon leaves mixed
with 1 tablespoon red wine vinegar
2 teaspoons tarragon vinegar
1 teaspoon Worcestershire sauce
½ cup whipped cream (measured after whipping)
1 lemon, cut into 4 slices as a garnish

* Csekonics saláta

1. Season the chicken breasts with salt and pepper and set them in a baking pan. Stir the paprika in the oil and spread over the breasts. Bake in a preheated 325 °F oven for about 40 minutes until cooked through. Cut about an inch off the ends of each breast. Cut the trimmed breasts crosswise into 4 slices each, cover and chill until serving time. Chop the trimmed ends and reserve.

2. Set aside 12 shrimp, cover and refrigerate. Chop the remaining shrimp. Toss the chopped shrimp with the chopped chicken in a 2-quart bowl, cover and refrigerate for at least 30 minutes.

3. Bring 4 cups of water to a boil in a 2-quart pan. Add the tomatoes and cook for about 1 minute until the skins crack. Plunge immediately into cold water. Peel and seed the tomatoes and cut into slices. Lay the tomatoes on a plate and season with salt and pepper. Cover and chill for at least 30 minutes.

4. Put aside a few washed and drained lettuce leaves, then tear up the rest into pieces of the same size. Remove the chicken-shrimp mixture from the refrigerator and toss with the lettuce. At the same time, remove the sliced chicken and whole shrimp and let them come to room temperature.

5. Mix the mayonnaise with salt and cayenne pepper to taste. Stir in the tarragon-vinegar mixture and the tarragon vinegar. Fold the whipped cream into the mayonnaise. Add half of the tomatoes to the chicken-shrimp mixture and then toss with the flavored mayonnaise.

6. Arrange the lettuce leaves on the plates and put the mixed salad on them. Divide the chicken slices, reserved shrimp and remaining tomato slices among the plates. Garnish each plate with a lemon slice.

Soups

Iced Honeydew Soup
with Tokaji Wine · 28

Veal Broth, Windsor Style · 30

Caraway-Seed Soup with Poached Eggs · 32

Mommy's Christmas Wine Soup · 33

His Majesty's, Franz Joseph I,
Favorite Soup · 35

Madame Rose's Crayfish Bisque · 37

Goulash Soup with Little Pinched Noodles · 39

Palóc Soup · 41

Young Wild Boar Soup with Tarragon · 43

Iced Honeydew Soup
with Tokaji Wine*

4 servings

1 honeydew melon (about 4 pounds)
3 tablespoons Tokaji aszú
or a sweet dessert wine of your choice
½ cup semisweet white wine,
such as Gundel Tokaji Hárslevelű
3 tablespoons heavy cream
1 bunch fresh mint, as garnish

1. Cut the top of the melon as shown in the photo.
Remove the seeds with a spoon.

* Jegelt dinnyeleves tokaji borral ízesítve

2. Cut 16 balls from the honeydew melon with a melon baller. Put the balls into a cup, add the Tokaji aszu and refrigerate.

3. Scrape the remaining melon flesh into a 4-quart bowl. Refrigerate the melon rind intact. Add the wine and cream to the melon flesh, cover and refrigerate until chilled. Puree the melon in a blender or food processor and refrigerate again for at least 1 hour until chilled.

4. Pour the refrigerated soup into the chilled rind, add the melon balls and the Tokay aszu accumulated in the cup into the soup. Present the soup in the rind on the table, garnished with fresh mint. Serve in chilled cups.

For generations, sweet-and-sour fruit soups have been made in Hungarian kitchens. Transylvanian Princess Anna Bornemisza's cookbook, published in 1680, contains such soups as Caper Soup with Black Sea-Grapes, Butter Soup with Raisins, and Sweet Wine Soup, to mention only a few. This soup is ideal for a hot summer day.

Veal Broth, Windsor Style*

4 servings

2 pounds meaty veal bones
1 pound veal leg, bone in
10 ounces ground veal
2 large egg whites
1 tomato, quartered
1 carrot, peeled
1 turnip, peeled
1 stalk celery, washed
1 small onion
1 small mushroom, cleaned
6 black peppercorns
1 walnut-sized piece
of fresh ginger, peeled
Salt
3 tablespoons dry sherry

1. Bring 2 quarts water to a boil in a 4-quart pot. Add the veal bones and leg and let the water return to a boil. Drain and rinse the bones and leg with cold water.

2. Mix the ground veal, egg whites and tomato with 1 quart of water in a 4-quart pot. Add the scalded bones and leg, another 1 quart of water, carrot, turnip,

* Borjú erőleves Windsor módra

celery, onion, mushroom, peppercorns and ginger. Bring to a boil over medium heat, stirring constantly with a wooden spoon. When the soup starts boiling, stop stirring, reduce the heat and simmer for 3 hours, seasoning to salt if desired. Let the soup rest for 5 minutes. Lift the veal leg from the soup and set aside. Strain through a well-wrung, damp linen cloth into a 1½-quart pot. Discard the vegetables, meat, and bones.

3. Skim the fat from the surface of the soup. Rinse the veal leg with cold water, cut the pure white meat from the bone (discarding any gristle or fat) and cut the meat into 2-inch-long pieces. Add the meat and sherry to the broth. Gently reheat until hot. Serve in warm cups.

This soup was served by Károly Gundel at his parents' wedding-anniversary party.

31

Caraway-Seed
Soup with Poached Eggs*

4 servings

2 tablespoons vegetable oil
1 tablespoon whole caraway seeds
2 tablespoons all-purpose flour
½ teaspoon sweet Hungarian paprika
2 cups chicken broth
Salt
4 large eggs

1. Heat oil in a 2½-quart pot. Add the caraway seeds and stir with a wooden spoon until the seeds begin to pop and crackle. Dust them with flour and continue stirring until the mixture turns sandy-colored.

2. Remove from the heat and add the paprika. Pour in 3 cups of water and the chicken broth. Season to taste with salt, bring to a boil, reduce the heat and simmer for 25 minutes. Strain the soup into a clean pot.

3. Just before serving, return the soup to the stove and bring to a simmer. While the soup is heating, crack the eggs one by one into small cups. As soon as the soup starts to boil, carefully slide the eggs into the simmer-

* Köménymagleves buggyantott tojással

ing soup, keeping them whole. Poach for just 2 minutes; the yolk will remain soft.

4. Serve in cups or bowls with 1 egg for each serving.

Without eggs, served only with toast, this is called "poor people's soup". This is a tasty soup, and when made with poached quail eggs, can be very elegant. If you make it with quail eggs, serve the soup in small cups.

Mommy's Christmas Wine Soup[*]

4 servings

2 cups semisweet white wine,
such as Gundel Tokaji Hárslevelű
4 cloves
1 allspice berry
1 small cinnamon stick
Zest of ½ lemon

* Mami karácsonyi borlevese

6 large egg yolks
6 tablespoons granulated sugar

1. Boil the wine, 2 cups of water, cloves, allspice, cinnamon stick and lemon zest in a saucepan. Simmer for 5 minutes and then remove the spices and lemon zest with a tea strainer or skimmer.

2. Whisk the egg yolks and sugar until foamy in a 1-quart saucepan. Add ¼ cup of the wine, whisking continuously. When incorporated, add the remaining wine and cook for 3 or 4 minutes longer, stirring constantly until the mixture lightens in color. (If you do not whisk continuously, the eggs will separate and turn into threads, as in egg-drop soup.) Serve hot.

It is traditional to serve a fragrant wine soup at Christmas, served after walking home in the crispy snow from midnight mass. This recipe has been passed down through generations in Hungarian families.

His Majesty's, Franz Joseph I, Favorite Soup[*]

4 servings

¼ cup unsalted butter
1 large potato, peeled and sliced
1 artichoke heart, sliced
½ stalk celery, sliced
½ leek, sliced
1 tablespoon all-purpose flour
2 cups chicken broth
1 cup milk
½ cup heavy cream
Salt and freshly ground
white pepper
2 ounces boiled,
smoked beef-tongue
1 small truffle

1. Melt the butter in a 2-quart pot. Add the potato, artichoke heart, celery, and leek and sauté over medium heat for 5 minutes. Dust with flour, stir and add the chicken broth, milk and cream. Season to taste with salt and pepper and simmer for 40 to 50 minutes, stirring frequently.

***Őfelsége I. Ferenc József császár és király kedvenc levese**

2. Pour the soup into a blender in batches, blending until smooth. Transfer each batch to a clean pot.

3. Cut the tongue and the truffle into very thin strips, the size of vermicelli.

4. Reheat the soup, if necessary, and serve it hot in heated cups, with the tongue and truffle pieces divided among each serving.

This recipe comes from an old cookbook discovered in Baden bei Wien around 1950. In the cookbook, which was the property of Franz Joseph's chef, the following remark was written beside the recipe: "His Majesty's favorite soup."

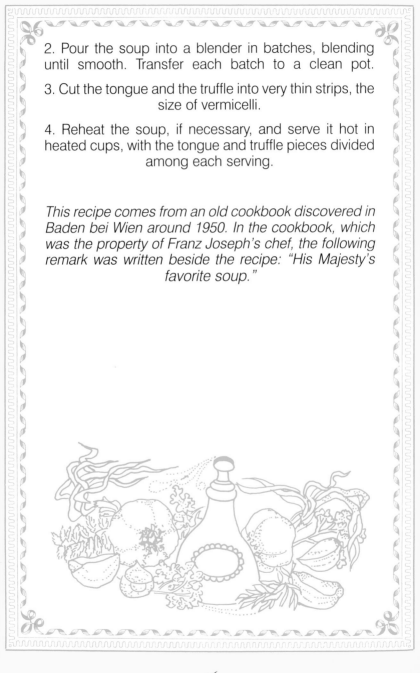

Madame Rose's Crayfish Bisque*

4 servings

Crayfish and Cooking Liquid

2 quarts chicken stock
1 bunch parsley, 1 teaspoon salt
2 pounds live crayfish

Filling

2 tablespoons cooked rice
2 tablespoons cooked green peas
1 large egg yolk
1 tablespoon grated Swiss cheese

Soup

2 tablespoons unsalted butter
1 small carrot, peeled and sliced
1 parsnip, peeled and sliced
1 stalk celery, sliced, 1 small onion, sliced
1 teaspoon crushed dried thyme
8 black peppercorns
1 small tomato, cut into half
4 tablespoons all-purpose flour
1 teaspoon Hungarian sweet paprika
1 cup dry white wine,
such as Gundel Tokaji Furmint
1 cup heavy cream, 2 tablespoons brandy

* Róza asszony ráklevese

37

Crayfish

1. Put the chicken stock, parsley and salt in a 3-quart pot and bring to a boil. Toss the crayfish, one by one, into the boiling stock and simmer for 5 minutes. Remove the crayfish with a skimmer and plunge them into cold water to cool. Strain the hot cooking water into another pot.

2. Remove the claws and the tails from the crayfish by twisting them off the bodies, and then remove the meat. Set aside 4 of the best-looking shells, selecting those that are approximately the same size; reserve the remaining shells. Thoroughly rinse the meat with cool water. Put the meat into the reserved, hot cooking water. After 5 minutes, remove the meat and cool it in cold water. Again, reserve the cooking water.

3. Wash the reserved shells thoroughly. Crush the remaining shells using a stone mortar and pestle and set aside

Filling

Mix the rice and the green peas with the egg yolk and grated cheese. Stuff the reserved crayfish shells with this mixture and set aside.

Soup

1. Melt the butter in a 4-quart saucepan and sauté the carrot, parsnip and celery, stirring constantly, for 5 or 6 minutes. Add the onion, tomato and thyme and pepper and sauté for 3 or 4 minutes longer until lightly browned.

2. Dust the vegetables with flour and paprika and mix well. Pour the reserved cooking water and wine into the pan. Add the crushed shells and simmer for 1 hour, stirring occasionally. Strain the soup through a fine-

mesh strainer into a clean pot. Discard the shells and vegetables.

3. Bring the soup to a boil, add the cream and the brandy and cook, stirring constantly, for 2 minutes to blend. Add the reserved crayfish meat and stuffed shells and heat just until heated through. Transfer the hot soup to a tureen and serve with one shell for each serving.

The actress Róza Laborfalvy was also an excellent cook. In 1848, she personally purchased crayfish and other delicacies at a market on the shores of the Danube market when she invited the novelist Mór Jókai and the poet Sándor Petőfi for dinner. The first course on her menu that evening was this soup, followed by the surprising announcement by Mór Jókai that he and Róza Laborfalvy were to be married.

Goulash Soup
with Little Pinched Noodles*

4 servings

3 tablespoons vegetable oil
2 onions, chopped
1¾ pounds beef, cut into ½-inch cubes
¼ teaspoon ground caraway seeds
2 small hot cherry peppers,
seeded and chopped
(1 of the peppers is optional)
1 clove garlic, crushed, Salt

* Gulyásleves csipetkével

1 tablespoon Hungarian sweet paprika
1 small carrot, peeled and diced
1 small stalk celery, diced
1 small parsnip, diced
1 small bunch fresh parsley
2 potatoes, cut into ½-inch cubes
1 tomato, peeled,
seeded and cut into ½-inch cubes
1 green bell pepper, diced
Little Pinched Noodles (see page 186.)

1. Heat the oil in a 3-quart pot and sauté the onions until golden. Add the meat, cover, and good slowly for 15 to 20 minutes so the meat can release its fat. Add the caraway seeds, 1 chopped cherry pepper, and garlic and season to taste with salt. Stir and then add 1 cup of water.

2. Simmer for 40 minutes, covered, until the meat begins to turn tender. Stir occasionally and add more water as necessary. The water should not evaporate.

3. Dust the meat with paprika, add the carrot, celery, parsnips and parsley and simmer for about 30 minutes until the meat is nearly tender. Add the potatoes, tomato, and pepper and 3½ cups of water. Simmer, uncovered, over low heat. When the potato is nearly tender, add half of the noodles and cook for about 5 minutes until both the pasta and potatoes are tender.

4. Serve hot, either in a soup tureen or in cups. Garnish with the remaining chopped cherry pepper, if desired.

There are more than 12 noted variations on goulash from Károly Gundel's repertoire. This recipe could be considered the classic one for goulash–if there is such a formula.

Palóc Soup[*]

4 servings

3 tablespoons vegetable oil
2 onions, finely chopped
1 teaspoon sweet Hungarian paprika
¾-pound roast-lamb shoulder blade
cut into ½-inch cubes
1 small clove garlic, crushed
¼ teaspoon ground caraway seeds
1 bay leaf, Salt
1 large potato, cut into ½-inch cubes
6 ounces green beans,
cut into ½-inch pieces
Pinch of baking soda
½ cup sour cream
2 tablespoons all-purpose flour
1 tablespoon chopped fresh dill

1. Heat the oil in a 2-quart pot and sauté the onions until golden. Remove the pot from the heat, add paprika and 2 cups water and stir. Return to low heat, add the lamb, garlic, caraway seeds, bay leaf and salt to taste and simmer, covered, for about 1 hour and 20 minutes until the meat is tender. Add more water as necessary; it should not evaporate.

* Palócleves

2. While meat is cooking, put the potato and 1 cup of lightly salted water in a saucepan and cook for 10 to 12 minutes until the potato is fork tender. Remove from the heat but do not drain.

3. Put the green beans, baking soda and 1 cup of lightly salted water in a saucepan and cook for 8 to 10 minutes until just tender. Do not overcook. (The baking soda helps keep the beans green.) Remove from the heat but do not drain.

4. In a cup, mix the sour cream and flour with ¼ cup water, stirring until smooth.

5. When the meat is tender, add the potato, the beans and their cooking water, and the sour cream mixture. Bring to a boil and cook for 5 minutes. Add more water if the soup is too thick. Remove bay leaf before serving. Garnish each serving with dill.

János Gundel, the founder of the Gundel dynasty, created this soup for Mikszáth, the Hungarian writer who often is referred to as the "Hungarian MarkTwain." The author expressed his desire for a soup which was like goulash–yet was not goulash. Mikszáth wrote about the Palóc people, inhabitants of northeastern Hungary, thus the name.

Young Wild Boar Soup with Tarragon[*]

4 servings

½ teaspoon sugar

3 tablespoons vegetable oil

2 onions, finely chopped

1 pound young wild-boar
shoulder blade or thigh meat,
or pork shoulder blades,
cut into ½-inch cubes

1 bay leaf

1 small clove garlic, crushed

Salt and freshly
ground black pepper

½ carrot, peeled and dice

1 parsnip, peeled and diced

½ stalk celery, diced

1 bay leaf

¼ lemon

1 tablespoon finely
chopped fresh tarragon

⅓ cup sour cream

⅓ cup heavy cream

1 tablespoon all-purpose flour

1 tablespoon prepared mustard

2 tablespoons chopped fresh parsley

* Tárkonyos vadmalacleves

1. Heat the sugar in a 2-quart pot until dark brown. Add the oil and onions and cook, stirring constantly, until the onion softens. Add the meat, bay leaf, and garlic and season with salt and pepper. Add 1 cup of water and simmer over low heat for about 30 minutes, covered. Add more water if necessary; do not let the water evaporate. Add the carrot, parsnip, celery, lemon, bay leaf, and tarragon and mix well. Add 2 cups of water and simmer for about 1½ hours until the meat is tender.

2. Mix the sour cream, heavy cream, flour and mustard in a small mixing bowl until well blended. Add to the soup and stir well with a wooden spoon. Simmer for about 5 minutes over low heat. Add enough water to make a properly thick meat soup.

3. Remove the bay leaf before serving. Garnish each serving with parsley.

The combination of tarragon, sour cream and heavy cream make this soup a piquant, appetizing dish, which is a worthy beginning to a characteristically rich Hungarian feast.

Warm First Courses

Stuffed Mushrooms · 46

Frogs' Legs in Parsley Sauce · 49

Snails with Garlic Cheese · 51

Rich Man's Purse Filled
with Paprika Chicken · 54

Grassalkovich Crêpe · 57

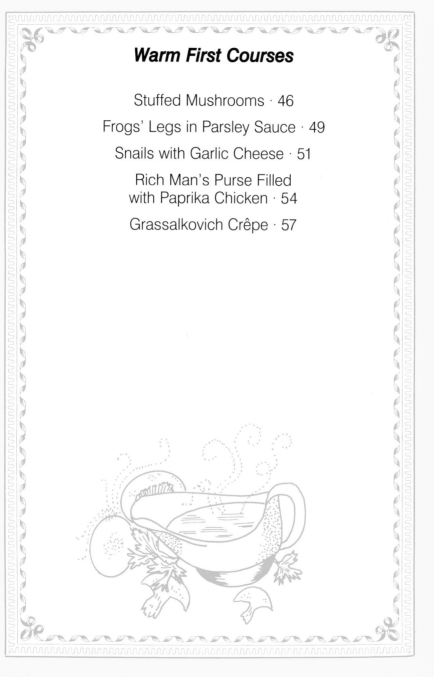

Stuffed Mushrooms*

4 servings

1 pound fresh
champignon mushrooms,
1½-inch diameter caps
3 tablespoons unsalted butter
1 heaped tablespoon chopped onion
1 heaped tablespoon chopped
fresh parsley
Salt and black pepper
4 tablespoons dried bread crumbs
2 tablespoons all-purpose flour
2 large egg yolks

* Gomba gombában

½ cup dry red wine

1 cup Brown Veal Stock
(see page 179.)

2 teaspoons cornstarch
or potato starch

Filling

1. Stem the mushrooms. Put aside the 8 nicest caps and chop up the rest, together with the stems. Put the chopped mushrooms in a colander set on a shallow dish and press the liquid from the mushrooms with a clean cloth. Reserve the accumulated liquid.

2. In a 6-inch frying pan, melt 1½ tablespoons of butter over medium heat. Sauté the onion until golden brown. Add the chopped mushrooms and sauté for 1 minute. Add the parsley, salt and pepper. Reduce the heat, add the bread crumbs and flour and cook for 5 more minutes, stirring constantly.

3. Remove the pan from the heat and let cool for 3 or 4 minutes. Add the egg yolks to the mushroom mixture and stir 2 for minutes. Set aside.

Sauce

1. Boil the wine in a ½-quart saucepan until it is reduced by half. Add the stock and the reserved mushroom liquid and boil until reduced by half. Season with salt and pepper.

2. Stir 1 teaspoon of cornstarch into a little water (a tablespoon or two) in a small cup until smooth and stir into the sauce. Boil for 3 to 4 minutes while constantly stirring, and then strain through a fine sieve. Cover and keep warm.

To Stuff and Fry

1. Cut a thin slice from the top of the reserved mushroom caps so that they can sit evenly on a flat surface. Reserve the slices. Turn the caps over and fill with the mushroom filling, using a teaspoon. Cover the filling with the reserved mushroom slices.

2. In a 6-inch frying pan, heat the remaining butter over medium heat. Add the mushrooms to the pan, stuffed side up, and sauté for approximately 3 minutes until the base turns golden. Carefully remove the mushrooms and place them, stuffed side up, in a round baking dish, large enough for the mushrooms to fit comfortably.

3. Bake the stuffed mushrooms in a preheated 350 °F oven until the tops turn slightly brown. Check after 3 minutes. Pour the sauce over the mushrooms and serve hot.

This dish figures since the opening of the New Gundel on the carte de jour. The combination of fresh champignon mushrooms, parsley and onions seasoned with freshly ground pepper results in a light, tasty hot entrée.

Frogs' Legs
in Parsley Sauce[*]

4 servings

16 pair frogs' legs with thighs
Salt
4 tablespoons all-purpose flour
3 tablespoons unsalted butter
¼ pound champignon mushrooms,
stemmed and sliced
2 tablespoons chopped fresh parsley
½ cup chicken broth
1 cup heavy cream
1 cup green peas, cooked
½ cup of cooking water reserved
Freshly ground white pepper
2 cups steamed rice
Vegetable oil
1 bunch fresh parsley

Frogs Legs and Thighs

1. Wash the frogs legs and thighs. Cut a slit in the calf meat and pass the other leg of the pair through each calf so that the thighs will maintain their shape during cooking.

2. Salt the frogs legs and thighs and roll them in flour. In a 7-inch frying pan, heat 2 tablespoons of butter and

* Kecskebékacombok petrezselymes mártásban

sauté for 2 minutes on each side. Add the mushrooms to the pan and saute for 2 or 3 minutes longer. Sprinkle with 1 tablespoon of chopped parsley and the remaining flour and stir well. Add the chicken broth, cream and the reserved cooking water from the peas. Cook over medium heat for 5 or 6 minutes. Season to taste with salt and pepper.

Rice and Peas

In a 7-inch frying pan, heat 1 tablespoon of butter over medium heat and sauté the cooked peas for a minute or so. Sprinkle with the remaining tablespoon of parsley, stir, and then mix with the steamed rice.

Fried Parsley

Trim the stems from the parsley bunch. Pour oil into a deep frying pan to a depth of about 1 inch and heat over medium-high heat until very hot. Add the parsley and fry for a few seconds until crisp. Lift from the oil with a slotted spoon and drain on paper towels.

To Serve

Press the peas and rice firmly into four lightly oiled 3- or 4-inch savarin molds (forms with a hole in the middle). Turn out onto each plate. Spoon the mushrooms and frogs legs and thighs into the middle of the rice ring. Garnish with fried parsley.

This is a light and tasty entrée. At Gundel's we are using Hungarian frogs: though they are smaller than the imported ones, their thighs are much tastier.

Snails
with Garlic Cheese*
4 servings

Snails

48 large live snails
1 pound salt
4 porcelain snail plates

Cooking Liquid

Salt
2 cups dry white wine
1 teaspoon caraway seeds
8 cloves garlic
10 black peppercorns
1 small bunch fresh parsley
Leaves from a small bunch of celery

Garlic Cheese

½ cup unsalted butter, softened
4 ounces smoked firm cheese,
grated, such as smoked Cheddar or Gouda
1 large egg yolk
1 teaspoon crushed garlic
1 teaspoon anchovy paste
1 tablespoon finely chopped fresh parsley

* Forró csigák kőtálban fokhagymás sajttal

1 teaspoon chopped celery leaves
1 teaspoon finely chopped fresh thyme
Salt
½ teaspoon freshly ground white pepper

Snails

1. Put the snails in a plastic bag with holes poked in it to let them breathe (suffocation will destroy their flavor). Store them in a cool place (a refrigerator or a cool basement will work) and leave them to starve for 4 days.

2. Wash the snails well in cold water. In a large pot, bring 3 quarts of water to a boil and boil the snails for 30 minutes. Drain and rinse with cold water. Prick a sharp needle into each snail shell and with a twisting motion remove the snails.

3. Put the snail meat in a 3-quart bowl. Add the pound of salt and rub the snails and salt between your palms to remove the mucus. To check, rinse a few snails under running water. If there is no yellow mucus left on the snails, they are well cleaned. Rinse the snails well to remove all the salt.

Cooking Liquid

In a large pot, bring 3 quarts of water to a boil. Add a little salt and the wine. Wrap the caraway seeds, garlic, peppercorns, parsley and celery leaves in cheesecloth, secure tightly and drop into the water. Add the snails and cook over low heat for 3 hours. Let the snails cool in the cooking water.

Garlic Cheese

1. Mix the butter, cheese, egg yolk, garlic, anchovy paste, parsley, celery leaves and thyme. Season to taste

with salt and pepper. Put the mixture on aluminum foil and roll into a cylinder. Refrigerate for 1 hour.

2. Heat porcelain snail plates in a preheated 300 °F oven for 10 minutes. Press the snails well with your hands to squeeze out excess liquid. Remove the snail plates from the oven, raise the oven temperature to 350 °F. Put 2 snails in each indentation in the plates. Unfold the chilled cheese-butter roll and cut 24 slices. Top each pair of snails with a cheese-butter slice and bake for 6 to 8 minutes until the butter melts and sizzles and the snails are heated through.

3. Serve hot with toast.

It may be easier to use canned snails, which do not require soaking and boiling. This way, you can make the entire dish on the day you plan to serve it.

Rich Man's Purse
Filled with Paprika Chicken*

4 servings

Paprika chicken

1 tablespoon vegetable oil

1 onion, finely diced

1 tablespoon sweet Hungarian paprika

½ chicken (1 pound),
cut into 4 pieces, skinned

1 tomato, peeled, seeded,
cut into ¼-inch cubes

1 green bell pepper,
cut into ¼-inch cubes

* Gazdag ember batyuja paprikás csirkével töltve

1 small hot cherry pepper,
seeded and diced, optional
Salt
½ cup plus 2 tablespoons sour cream
½ cup heavy cream
1 teaspoon all-purpose flour
Salt and freshly ground white pepper

Crêpes

¾ cup all-purpose flour
1 large egg
½ cup milk
⅓ cup seltzer water
Salt
Approximately ¼ cup vegetable oil
4 long chives, dipped in very hot water
for 1 second and drained

Paprika Chicken

1. In a large pot, heat the oil. Sauté the onion until golden brown. Remove from the heat, add ½ cup of water and 2 teaspoons of sweet paprika and mix well. Return to the stove on low heat. Add the chicken, tomato and peppers and season to taste with salt. Cook, covered, for about 40 minutes until the meat is tender. Remove the chicken parts and set aside. In a bowl, mix ½ cup of sour cream, the heavy cream and the flour. Add the mixture to the sauce and bring to a boil.

2. Bone the chicken and cut the meat into small pieces. Mix with 1 tablespoon of the sauce, the remaining 2 tablespoons of sour cream, the remaining

teaspoon of paprika, and season to taste with salt and pepper in a mixing bowl. Return to the pot and bring to a boil. Boil for 2 minutes, remove from the heat and set aside to cool slightly.

Crêpes

1. Whisk together the flour, egg, milk, seltzer water and salt to taste until smooth. Heat a frying pan, smear it with oil and pour the crêpe batter into the hot pan so that it thinly and evenly covers the bottom of the pan. Turn the crepe over after approximately 15 seconds. Cook for a few more seconds and lift from the pan. Add more oil as necessary and cook the remaining batter to make 4 crêpes.

2. Divide the filling into 4 portions and spoon into the center of each crêpe. Join the edges of each crepe to form a small bundle, crimping it at the top and fastening with a toothpick. Tie each bundle around its center with a softened chive and transfer to a lightly oiled baking dish. Heat in a preheated 350 °F oven for 4 or 5 minutes until crispy.

Both the paprika chicken and the crêpe are traditional dishes of the Hungarian kitchen. Their combination in the Rich man's purse is a quite new, tasty hot entrée. It is a stylish introduction to a satisfying lunch or dinner "Hungarian style".

Grassalkovich Crêpe*

4 servings

Lecsó

1 tablespoon vegetable oil

1 slice bacon, cut into 1-inch pieces

1 heaped tablespoon
finely chopped onion

1 teaspoon sweet Hungarian paprika

2 ounces smoked sausage,
cut into 1-inch pieces

3 yellow bell peppers,
cut into 2-inch dice

1 tomato, peeled, seeded,
cut into 2-inch dice

Salt

Duck Liver

Salt

6 ounces duck livers, cut into 4 slices

Pinch of crumbled dried marjoram

1 tablespoon all-purpose flour

1 teaspoon vegetable oil

4 long chives, dipped in very hot water
for 1 second and drained

Red, green and yellow bell peppers,
diced, optional, for garnish

* Grassalkovich palacsinta

Paprika Sauce

1 tablespoon vegetable oil
1 onion, finely diced, 2 cup water
1 tablespoon sweet Hungarian paprika
1 chicken (2 pounds),
cut into pieces, skin removed
1 tomato, peeled, seeded, cut into ¼-inch cubes
1 green bell pepper, cut into ¼-inch cubes
1 small hot cherry pepper, seeded and diced, optional
Salt
½ cup sour cream, ½ cup heavy cream
1 teaspoon all-purpose flour
Salt and freshly ground white pepper

Crêpes

See page 56.

Lecsó

In a frying pan, heat the oil and fry the bacon until it begins to brown. Add the onion and cook until golden brown. Remove from heat and mix well with the sweet paprika. Add the sausage, peppers, tomato and salt to taste. Simmer, covered, for 8 to 10 minutes on medium heat. Remove from the heat and keep warm.

Duck Livers

Salt the duck livers, sprinkle with crumbled marjoram and roll in flour. Heat the oil in a frying pan over medium heat and sauté the duck livers for 1 or 2 minutes on each side, depending on thickness of the slices, until lightly browned.

Paprika Sauce

In a large pot, heat the oil. Sauté the onion until golden brown. Remove from the heat, add the water and 2 teaspoons of sweet paprika and mix well. Return to the stove on low heat. Add the chicken, tomato, and peppers and season to taste with salt. Cook, covered, for about 40 minutes until the meat is tender. Remove the chicken parts and set aside for another use. In a bowl, mix the sour cream, heavy cream and the flour. Add to the sauce and bring to a boil. Stir well and remove from the heat. Cover and keep warm.

To Serve

1. Divide the sausage lecsó into 4 portions and spoon each into the center of each crêpe. Place 1 slice of duck liver on top of the lecsó. Join the edges of each crêpe to form a small bundle, crimping it at the top and fastening with a toothpick. Tie each bundle around its center with a softened chive and transfer to a lightly oiled baking dish. Heat in a preheated 300 °F oven for 3 or 4 minutes until crispy.

2. Pool the paprika sauce in the middle of 4 warm plates and place the bundles on the sauce. Garnish with diced peppers, if desired.

When Count Antal Grassalkovich entertained Empress Maria Theresa for dinner in his Baroque Gödöllő castle, he asked his chef for a "magnificently rich and elegant" first course, which explains how this dish of crêpes filled with sausage lecsó and sautéed duck livers was created.

59

Goose Liver

Bugac Goose Liver Flavored
with Tokaji Aszú · 61

Goose Liver
in the Traditional Way · 63

Apple and Goose Liver Sandwich · 65

Smoked Goose Liver
(suitable as either first or main course) · 67

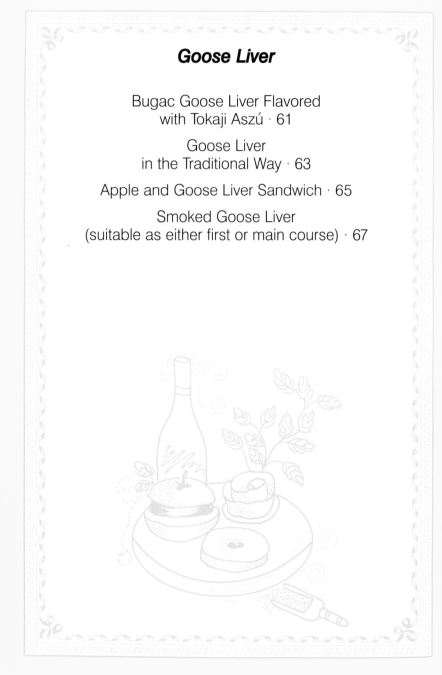

Bugac Goose Liver Flavored with Tokaji Aszú*

4 servings

Goose Liver

1 pound fresh goose liver
Salt and freshly ground white pepper to taste
¼ cup Gundel Tokaji aszú
or other sweet dessert wine of your choice

Tokaji Jelly

2 teaspoons unflavored powdered gelatin
⅓ cup chicken broth
¼ cup Gundel Tokaji aszú
or other sweet dessert wine of your choice
Red or green seedless grapes, for serving
Lightly toasted white bread, cut into triangles,
crusts trimmed, for serving

Goose Liver

1. Lay the liver, rounded side up, on an 8-inch porcelain plate and remove both the thick and thin veins. Separate the liver into its two halves and spread them so that they cover the plate. Remove any remaining veins, if necessary. Sprinkle with salt, pepper and the Tokaji aszú.

2. Fold the liver into its original shape and flatten it slightly by tapping it a few times with the palm of your

* Bugaci libamáj tokaji aszúval ízesítve

61

hand. Transfer it to a sheet of aluminum foil large enough to encase the liver, sprinkle any Tokaji aszú that accumulated on the plate over the liver, and wrap the foil to make a secure package. Refrigerate for 10 to 12 hours to give the salt, pepper and Tokaji aszú time to penetrate the goose liver.

3. Put the goose liver in a ½-quart heatproof porcelain or glass dish, cover with foil and then set the dish in a larger roasting pan. Put the roasting pan on the center rack of a preheated 200 °F oven, add enough hot water to the roasting pan to come about a third of the way up the sides of the dish and cook for about 2 hours. Remove the roasting pan from the oven and let the liver cool to room temperature. Refrigerate, covered, for several hours until chilled, or for up to 24 hours.

Tokaji Jelly

1. In a coffee cup, sprinkle the gelatin over 2 tablespoons of warm water. In a ½-quart saucepan, bring the broth and Tokaji aszú to a boil. Add the gelatin, stir well and bring to a boil again. Remove from the heat and let cool to room temperature.

2. When cool, pour into a small, shallow metal dish large (the liquid should be the depth of ½ to 1 inch) and refrigerate for 3 or 4 hours to set.

To Serve

Remove the goose liver from the dish and using a thin-bladed knife, slice thin. Plunge the knife into warm water and wipe dry between each slice. Arrange the slices on a platter or individual plates. Cut the jelly into 1-inch cubes and use to garnish the liver. Serve with the grapes and toast.

Goose Liver
in the Traditional Way*

4 servings as main dish
8 servings as first course

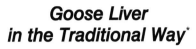

3 pounds goose fat with skin, diced
1 tablespoon milk
1½ pounds fresh goose liver
Salt to taste
2 red onions, halved
3 cloves garlic, crushed
1 green bell pepper,
halved and seeded
Sliced tomatoes, sliced red
or yellow peppers,
and sliced leeks, for garnish
Freshly sliced bread, for serving

1. In a frying pan, combine the goose fat with 2 table-spoons of water and cook, stirring constantly, over medium heat until the fat begins to render and the cubes turn yellow. Add the milk, taking care it does not spatter when it hits the hot fat. Stir to mix and then strain the rendered fat through a sieve into a 2-quart saucepan, pressing on the cracklings to extract as

* Libamáj zsírjában sütve hagyományos módon

much fat as possible. Let the fat cool until warm. Set the cracklings aside, spread on a flat tray or plate to cool. When cool, cover and set aside in a cool, dry place. (Do not refrigerate.)

2. Sprinkle the liver with salt and then put it in the warm goose fat. Add the onions, garlic and pepper and fry over medium heat for 20 to 25 minutes, depending on the size of the liver. To check for doneness, prick the thickest part of the liver with a needle or slender metal skewer; if no liquid escapes, it is done. Transfer the liver to a 1-quart porcelain bowl.

3. After removing the liver, continue cooking until onions are cooked through. Strain the fat from the pan over the liver so that the liver is completely covered with fat. Reserve the onions for another use or discard. Let the liver and fat cool to room temperature, cover and refrigerate until chilled and the fat solidifies. (Covered with fat and refrigerated, the liver will keep for several weeks, although is best if consumed within one week.)

To Serve

Scrape the fat from the liver and slice the liver into ½-inch slices. Reserve the fat. Serve the liver garnished with the tomatoes, peppers and leeks. Put the fat in a separate bowl, sprinkle with paprika and the reserved cracklings. Serve the fat with the bread and a little salt.

You can also serve the liver hot with mashed potatoes made with onions (see page 190.) and Fried Crisp Onion Rings (see page 191.).

Apple and Goose Liver Sandwich*

4 servings

4 red apples, such as Jonathans
2 tablespoons unsalted butter
½ pound goose liver (4 slices)
Salt and freshly ground
white pepper to taste

Apples

Cut the apple horizontally into three parts to form rings. Remove the cores. In a small frying pan, melt 1 tablespoon of butter and fry the apple rings for about 2 minutes, turning, until lightly browned. (Do not cut the apples until ready to fry.)

* Alma- és libamáj szendvics

Goose Liver

1. Sprinkle the liver lightly with salt and pepper. In a frying pan, melt the remaining tablespoon of butter and sauté the goose liver slices for about 2 minutes. Transfer the slices to a roasting pan and roast in a preheated 350 °F oven for 3 or 4 minutes until they turn a golden color.

2. Place one slice of liver between the top and bottom slice of each apple

To Serve

Lay the remaining 4 center apple rings on a platter and put the goose liver sandwiches next to them. Serve hot.

The harmonious balance of Hungarian goose liver and apples lends this dish a delicate and interesting character.

Smoked
Goose Liver*

4 servings as main course
8 servings as first course

1½ pounds fresh goose liver
Salt to taste
About 1 cup hot coals from the grill
(from the grill)
2 cups soaked cherry-wood chips

1. Sprinkle the goose liver slices with salt and lay them
on a metal roasting rack set in a roasting pan. Put 2 or
3 hot coals in a cast-iron skillet and spread about a

* Cseresznyefa füstjén készült libamáj

cup of the wood chips over them. Put the frying pan on the bottom of a preheated 200 °F oven.

2. Set the roasting pan on the middle rack of the oven and bake for 1 hour and 45 minutes. Check the smoke regularly, adding more chips or a little water as necessary to keep the oven smoky. About halfway through cooking, replenish the hot coals and chips.

3. Serve the liver hot as a main dish in one piece garnished with Mashed Potatoes with Onion (see page 190.) or Crisp Fried Onion Rings (see page 191.).

4. Serve the liver cold as a first course with toasted slices of bread

This recipe is for the cook who has a great exhaust system; it should not be attempted in the average home kitchen. When discussing how to enrich Gundel's menu with George Lang, he suggested smoking the goose liver. The idea was followed by action: I went directly to the kitchen and made a fire with cherry wood chips and soon presented this dish for tasting. It has been a favorite Gundel specialty ever since. If you want to try this at home, use a smoker or a kettle grill (or any grill with a good cover) and smoke the liver outdoors, scattering the wood chips over the hot coals and keeping the lid firmly in place, with the vents partially open, during smoking.

Fish

Fillet of Pike-Perch, Gundel Style · 70

Fillet of Pike-Perch, Kárpáti Style · 73

Trout with Whipped Yogurt with Dill · 76

Poached Trout Fillet from Szilvásvárad
with Wild Mushroom Sauce · 78

Fisherman's Soup, Gundel style · 81

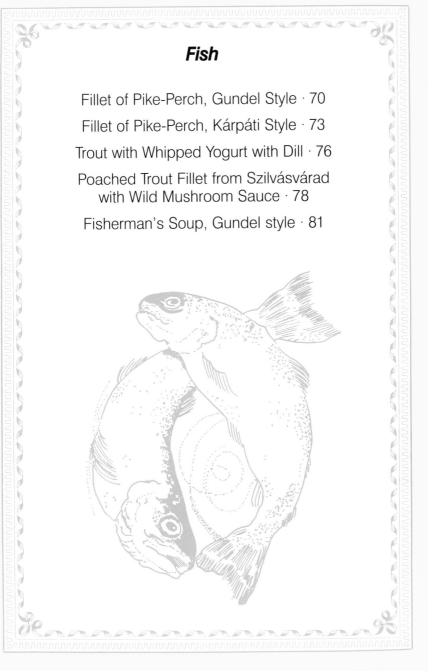

Fillet of Pike-Perch, Gundel Style[*]

4 servings

Vegetable Pearls

2 potatoes, peeled, 2 carrots, peeled
2 zucchinis
1 tablespoon unsalted butter
1 heaped tablespoon chopped
fresh parsley, Salt

Sauce

1 cup Fish Stock (see page 179.),
made from the pike-perch bones
¼ cup dry white wine
2 cups heavy cream, Salt

[*] *Fogasfilé Gundel módra*

Spinach

1½ pounds fresh spinach,
tough stems removed, washed
Pinch of baking soda
1 tablespoon unsalted butter
Salt and freshly ground white pepper

Fish

1¾ pounds boneless pike-perch,
cut into 4 slices
Salt
2 tablespoons all-purpose flour
⅓ cup vegetable oil

Vegetable pearls

1. Using a small melon scoop, hollow pearls from the potatoes, carrots and zucchini. Bring 2 small saucepans of water to a boil over high heat. Add the potatoes to one and the carrots to the other and cook for about 10 minutes until tender. A few minutes before the vegetables are done, bring a third saucepan of water to a boil and cook the zucchini for about 1 minute until tender.

2. Drain all 3 vegetables and mix together in one strainer. Melt the butter in a small frying pan. Add the vegetables and toss to coat. Add the parsley, season to taste with salt and cook over medium heat for about 3 minutes, tossing, until heated through. Cover and keep warm.

Sauce

In a ½-quart saucepan, combine the fish stock and wine, bring to a boil over medium heat and cook until reduced by about a third. In a separate, 1-quart saucepan, bring the cream to a boil over medium-high heat and cook until reduced by half. Slowly pour the stock into the cream, stirring to mix. Season to taste with salt, bring to a boil and cook for about 5 minutes until slightly thickened. Cover to keep warm.

Spinach

1. In a large pot, bring about 2½ quarts of water and the baking soda to a boil over high heat. Add the spinach and cook for about 2 minutes. Drain, rinse under cool water and then squeeze out the excess moisture.

2. In a saucepan, melt the butter. Add the spinach, season with salt and pepper, and cook gently for 2 minute until heated through.

Fish

Sprinkle the fish fillets lightly with salt and roll in flour. Heat the oil in a large, deep frying pan. Fry the fish for 6 or 7 minutes, turning one, until opaque and cooked through. Serve immediately.

To Serve

Divide the hot spinach among 4 warm plates. Pour the sauce around the spinach and arrange the vegetable pearls on the sauce. Lay the fried fish fillets on top of the spinach.

At Gundel this dish is made with fogas, a fish that lives only in Lake Balaton, a large lake in Hungary well known for the delicious fish. Fogas is related to the pike and perch family. You may use perch in this recipe, or any other white-fleshed fish, such as yellow (also known as walleye) pike.

Fillet of Pike-Perch, Kárpáti Style*

4 servings

Side dish

4 large potatoes, peeled, Salt
1 tablespoon unsalted butter
2 tablespoons chopped fresh parsley

Sauce

1 cup Fish Stock (see page 179.)
¼ cup dry white wine
2 cups heavy cream, Salt
3 tablespoons finely chopped dill

Crayfish

1½ pounds live crayfish

* Fogasfilé Kárpáti módra

1 small bunch fresh dill, for the cooking liquid
2 teaspoons salt
2 tablespoons unsalted butter

Mushrooms

10 ounces champignon mushrooms
1 tablespoon unsalted butter
Salt and freshly ground white pepper

Fish

1¾ pound boneless pike-perch,
cut into 4 slices, Salt
2 ounces all-purpose flour, ⅓ cup vegetable oil

Side dish

Cut the potatoes into 8 barrel-shaped pieces (see photo). Put the potatoes in a ½-gallon pot and add enough water to cover by 2 to 3 inches. Bring to a boil and cook until tender. Pour off the water, and in the same pot, melt the butter, add the parsley and gently toss the potatoes to coat with butter and parsley. Cover to keep warm.

Sauce

In a ½-quart saucepan, combine the fish stock and wine, bring to a boil over medium heat and cook until reduced by about a third. In a separate, 1-quart saucepan, bring the cream to a boil over medium-high heat and cook until reduced by half. Slowly pour the stock into the cream, stirring to mix. Add the dill and heat gently, stirring until the sauce turns light green. Season to taste with salt. Cover to keep warm.

Crayfish

1. Put 2 cups of water, the dill and the salt in a 3-quart pot and bring to a boil. Toss the crayfish, one by one,

into the boiling water and simmer for 5 minutes. Remove the crayfish with a skimmer and plunge them into cold water to cool. Set aside the 4 best-looking crayfish for garnish. Remove the claws and tails from the remaining crayfish, by twisting them off the bodies, and then remove the meat.

2. In a small frying pan, melt the butter over medium heat. Add the crayfish meat and cook, stirring, for 2 minutes. Cover and keep warm.

Mushrooms

Reserve 4 whole mushroom caps to use as garnish and set aside. Chop the remaining mushrooms, stems included. In a frying pan, melt the butter. Add the chopped mushrooms, season with salt and pepper and cook for 3 minutes, stirring occasionally. Drain in a colander before serving.

Fish

Sprinkle the fish fillets lightly with salt and roll in flour. Heat the oil in a large, deep frying pan. Fry the fish for 6 or 7 minutes on each side and serve immediately. At the same time, fry the reserved mushroom caps, stem side up, until lightly browned. Serve immediately.

To Serve

Divide the dill sauce among 4 hot plates and set the fried fish fillets and the mushrooms on top. Put the crayfish meat on one side and the mushroom caps on the other. Arrange 2 potato barrels and a whole crayfish on each plate.

In contrast with an older recipe, this one separates the fish, the whole mushrooms, the crayfish and the potatoes on the plate to create an aesthetically appealing dish.

Trout with Whipped Yogurt and Dill*

4 servings

1 cup plain yogurt
2 large egg yolks
¼ teaspoon confectioners' sugar
3 heaped tablespoons
finely chopped fresh dill
Salt
Four 10-ounce trout, cleaned,
head removed,
filleted but attached at the tail
3 heaped tablespoons
all-purpose flour
½ cup vegetable oil
4 large egg whites
1 small head broccoli, trimmed
1 carrot
1 parsnip
2 mushrooms
1 zucchini
2 tablespoons unsalted butter

1. Drape a piece of cheesecloth over 2 coffee mugs, allowing it a little slack. Secure the cheesecloth to the

* Pisztráng kapros joghurthab alatt sütve

cups with rubber bands. Divide the yogurt and put half on each piece of cheesecloth and refrigerate for 3 hours to give the yogurt time to drain. Scrape the thickened yogurt into a bowl and discard the liquid. Add the egg yolks, sugar and 2 tablespoons of dill to the yogurt, stir to mix and season to taste with salt.

2. Sprinkle the inside of the trout with 2 tablespoons of dill and season with salt. Fold fillets together and then roll the fish in the flour. In a large frying pan, heat the oil over medium-high heat. Add the trout and fry for about 3 minutes on each side. Transfer to a baking dish large enough to hold all 4 in a single layer.

3. Whisk the egg whites until foamy. Add the yogurt mixture and stir gently to mix. Pour over the trout and bake in a preheated 325 °F oven for about 8 minutes until heated through.

4. Meanwhile, cut the broccoli into florets and the carrot, parsnip, mushrooms and zucchini into pieces of equal size. Steam the carrots and parsnips for 10 minutes and the broccoli florets, zucchini and mushrooms for 5 minutes. In a large frying pan, melt the butter and add the vegetables. Add the parsley and toss to coat with butter and parsley. Season with salt and cook for about 2 minutes until heated through. Serve the trout with the vegetables.

This recipe comes from George Lang and although it may have originated on the other side of the ocean, the light dish ended up on Gundel's menu. It is not as complicated as it may seem, and I recommend trying it at home.

Poached Trout Fillet from Szilvásvárad with Wild Mushroom Sauce*

4 servings

Trout bones and heads from 4 trout
1 small carrot, sliced
1 small stalk celery, sliced
1 small onion, sliced
2 bay leaves
8 black peppercorns
1 cup dry white wine
Salt
8 trout fillets, skinned
3 potatoes

* Szilvásváradi posírozott pisztrángfilé vörös boros vadgomba mártással

1 tablespoon unsalted butter
1 tablespoon chopped fresh parsley
4 servings Wild Mushroom Sauce
(see page 183.)

1. In a 1-gallon pot, combine the trout bones and heads, carrot, celery, onion, bay leaves and peppercorns. Add the wine and salt to taste. Add enough cold water to fill the pot three-quarters full and bring to a boil. Reduce the heat and simmer over medium heat for about 30 minutes.

2. Strain the fish stock through a cheesecloth into a 3-quart fish kettle or fish poacher.

3. Roll the trout filets into funnel shapes and fasten each with a toothpick so that they keep their shape during poaching.

4. Remove the poaching rack from the fish kettle or poacher and place the trout funnels on it. Dip it into the hot fish stock and then add enough water so that the liquid covers the fillets. Season with salt, if necessary.

5. Poach the fillets over medium heat for 8 to 10 minutes, taking care the liquid never boils. Poaching time is important; if you hold the trout in the stock too long, they will be dry.

6. Remove the filets and the strainer from the stock.

7. With a small melon baller, scoop pearls from the potatoes. Transfer to a sauceapn and add enough water to cover by 2 or 3 inches. Lightly salt and bring to a boil. Reduce the heat and cook until the potato pearls are tender. Drain. Add the butter to the pan and

toss the potatoes in the melting butter. Add the parsley and toss to coat.

To Serve

Divide the hot mushroom sauce among 4 shallow soup bowls or plates. Lay two pieces of poached trout fillet on the sauce. Remove the toothpicks. Scatter the potato pearls over the sauce.

If you don't have a fish kettle or poacher, use a pot. Remove the fillets with a skimmer from the fish stock. You may serve this dish with either white or a light red wine.

Fisherman's Soup, Gundel Style*

4 servings

10 ounces carp fillets
1 pound carp bones
1 pound catfish bones
10 ounces catfish fillets
10 ounces pike-perch fillets
3 onions
1 clove garlic, peeled and left whole
2 green bell peppers, halved and seeded
1 tomato, seeded and chopped
2 tablespoons sweet Hungarian paprika
Salt
Little Pinched Noodles (see page 186.)
1 hot cherry pepper, seeded and chopped, optional

1. Put the carp and catfish bones in a 1-gallon pot.

2. Wash and pat dry the carp, catfish and pike fillets. Lay the fillets skin-side down on a work surface and

**** Gundel halászlé***

cut into them, scoring to make 1-inch pieces without cutting through the skin. Set the scored fillets aside.

3. Pour 10 cups of water over the fish bones, bring to a boil, reduce heat and simmer, skimming any foam that rises to the surface. Add the onions, garlic clove, green peppers, tomatoes, 1 tablespoon of paprika and salt to taste. Simmer for about 1 hour until reduced by slightly more than half.

4. Strain through a strainer into a 1-gallon pot, pressing gently against the colander to release as much liquid as possible. Discard the bones and vegetables.

5. Put the fish fillets into fish stock and sprinkle with the remaining tablespoon of paprika, if needed (the flavor of the paprika should be faint). Simmer for 10 or 15 minutes.

To Serve

1. Cook the noodles separately in salted water and add to the soup just before serving.

2. Serve the soup in a soup tureen or in individual bowls or cups. Serve the chopped cherry pepper on the side as garnish. When ladling the soup, take care not to break apart the fillets more than necessary.

Károly Gundel, who worked for the Ritz in Paris before opening Gundel in Budapest, asked his chef to prepare this traditional fisherman's soup using a number of different fish, as he had experienced it in Paris. I followed his example.

The fisherman's soup is a very popular dish since times immemorial all over Hungary. Following local

taste and customs there many variations. Along the Danube roe and milt is often added to the fillets of carp. Pasta is added to the Fisherman's Soup Kalocsa style. The Fisherman's Soup Baja style is enriched with vermicelli.

Along the Tisza River, on the Great Plain, the small fish are cooked, passed through a sieve and added to the soup, in wich fillets of carp, wels and sterlet are cooked.

Main Dishes

Breast of Squab
with Sauce Maltaise[*]

4 servings

Squab

4 young squab breasts

6 ounces duck liver, 1 tablespoon brandy

Salt and freshly ground white pepper to taste

1 small black truffle, thinly sliced

2 tablespoons olive oil, All-purpose flour

10 ounces commercial frozen puff pastry,
defrosted

1 large egg, lightly beaten

* Tavaszi galambmell máltai mártással

White Asparagus

1 pound white asparagus
½ teaspoon salt, ¼ teaspoon sugar

Green Asparagus

1 pound green asparagus
½ teaspoon salt, Pinch of baking soda
4 servings Maltaise Sauce (see page 184.)

Potatoes

2 baking potatoes, peeled and julienned
1 quart vegetable oil
1 pound small new potatoes
2 tablespoons unsalted butter, melted
1 tablespoon chopped fresh parsley

Squab

1. Bone and skin the squabs breasts and set the breasts aside. Roast the bones and the skin in a preheated 350 °F oven for about 30 minutes, stirring occasionally, until golden brown. Transfer to a small saucepan and add 2 cups of water. Bring to a boil, lower the heat and simmer for 30 minutes, skimming the foam that rises to the surface, or until reduced by about a quarter. Strain the broth into a bowl. Discard the bones and skin. Season the broth with salt, cover and set aside to keep warm. The broth can be refrigerated, if made ahead of time, and reheated just before serving.

2. Sprinkle the breasts with salt and pepper. Slice the duck liver into 8 slices and sprinkle them with brandy. Put 1 thin slice of truffle between 2 slices of duck liver and place them on one half of each breast. Fold the

other half over the liver and tie the breast closed with kitchen string.

3. In frying pan, heat the oil. Fry the breasts until lightly browned on each side. Set aside.

4. Sprinkle a work surface with flour and roll out the puff pastry into a large rectangle. Cut the pastry into 4 squares, each one large enough to cover a squab breast generously. Using a small sharp knife, make 3 or 4 rows of slits in the pastry squares about ½ inch apart. Make corresponding rows of slits to form a crosshatch pattern. Gently stretch the pastry squares to open the slits and create a net effect. (See photo.)

5. Drape one pastry net over each breast and tuck the edges under the breast. Brush the pastry with the beaten egg and put the breasts in a roasting pan large enough to hold them in a single layer. Refrigerate for about 20 minutes to chill the pastry.

6. Bake the breasts in a preheated 375 °F oven for 15 minutes and serve immediately.

White and Green Asparagus

1. Clean and peel the white asparagus, if necessary (see page 15.). Cut the cleaned asparagus into 2 inch lengths and transfer to a 1-quart saucepan. Add 2 cups of water, the salt and sugar and cook for over medium heat for 12 minutes. Strain, reserving the cooking liquid, and rinse the asparagus under cold water to stop the cooking.

2. Clean and peel the asparagus, if necessary (see page 15.). Cut the cleaned asparagus into 2 inch lengths and transfer to a 1-quart saucepan. Add 2 cups of water, the salt and sugar and cook for over medium

heat for 1 or 2 minutes if the asparagus are pencil thin and for 4 or 5 minutes if the asparagus are a little thicker. Strain, reserving the cooking liquid, and rinse the asparagus under cold water to stop the cooking.

3. Combine the green and white asparagus in a large pot or deep frying pan and pour the reserved cooking liquid over them. Reheat over medium-low heat until warm.

Potatoes

1. Put a quarter of the julienned potatoes in a small basket designed for making deep-fried potato baskets. Set the smaller basket on top of the potatoes to hold the basket shape. Heat the oil until very hot and deep fry the potato basket until crisp. Drain and set aside. Repeat with the remaining potatoes to make 4 baskets. (This can be done 1 hour ahead of time.)

2. In a saucepan of boiling, salted water, cook the new potatoes for about 15 minutes until tender. Drain and toss the potatoes with the butter and parsley.

To Serve

1. Fill the potato-baskets (see page 107.) with new potatoes and set one on each plate. Arrange the asparagus near them.

2. Cut the breasts diagonally in two. Separate the halves a little to expose a little filling and place on the plates. Put a spoonful of the warmed bone extract on top of the stuffed breasts. Spoon the Maltaise sauce over the asparagus.

Paprika Chicken,
According to the Lauder Family Recipe[*]

4 servings

Paprika Chicken

¼ cup vegetable oil
3 onions, finely chopped
3 cloves garlic, crushed
1 teaspoon sweet Hungarian paprika
2 whole chickens, quartered and trimmed
1 teaspoon salt
Hot Hungarian paprika to taste
1 tomato, peeled, seeded and cubed
2 green bell peppers, seeded and diced
Egg dumplings (see page 187.)

Garnish

1 tablespoon vegetable oil
1 yellow bell pepper, seeded and sliced
1 cup sour cream

Paprika Chicken

1. In a large pot, heat the oil over medium heat. Add the onions and sauté until golden brown. Remove from heat, add the garlic and the sweet paprika and stir well. Add 2 cups of water.

*** Paprikás csirke háziasan elkészítve,
a Lauder család receptje szerint**

2. Add the chicken pieces, salt and hot paprika to taste. Cover and cook over low heat for 20 minutes. Add the tomato and simmer for about 20 minutes longer or until the chicken is cooked through and tender. Lift the chicken from the pot and set aside.

4. Add the green peppers to the pot and simmer for about 15 minutes in the sauce.

5. When the chicken is cool enough to handle, remove the skin and cut the meat from the bones, keeping the breasts and thighs intact. Add the bones to the sauce and bring to a boil.

To Serve

1. In a frying pan, heat the oil. Add the yellow peppers and sauté for 3 minutes.

2. Place the egg dumplings on one side of each of 4 hot plates. Put a breast and thigh on each plate and pour the hot sauce over the meat. Garnish each plate with a dollop of sour cream and the yellow peppers.

The family of Ronald S. Lauder–the American co-proprietor of Gundel–comes from Sátoraljaújhely, Hungary. Paprika chicken had been the family's favorite dish for a very long time. This is Mr. Lauder's grandmother's recipe for paprika chicken, a dish that is very often included on Gundel's menu.

This is a lighter version of the paprika chicken because the sour cream is served separately. When preparing the paprika chicken in the traditional way, the sour cream is added to the juice and the two are mixed thoroughly.

Turkey with Chestnut Stuffing*

8 to 10 servings

Turkey
One 10-pound turkey
Salt and freshly ground white pepper
Vegetable oil

Stuffing
1 pound fresh chestnuts
5 slices bacon, cut into small pieces
2 tablespoons vegetable oil
2 onions, finely chopped
6 cups bread cubes, cut from day-old bread
1¼ cups chicken broth

* Gesztenyés töltött pulyka

6 large eggs, lightly beaten
1 tablespoon finely chopped fresh sage
2 tablespoons chopped fresh parsley
Salt and freshly ground white pepper

Gravy

1 teaspoon tomato puree
2 tablespoons all-purpose flour
Fried Quince
5 large quince or firm apples, scrubbed
4 tablespoons unsalted butter, melted
5 cloves
2 tablespoons confectioners' sugar
¼ cup unsalted butter
8 servings Potato Croquettes (see page 189.)
3 ounces slivered almonds
24 whole peppercorns, Vegetable oil

Turkey

Wash and dry the turkey to prepare it for roasting. Separate the skin from the meat on the breast starting from the neck, so that you can insert some stuffing under the skin. Sprinkle inside and out with salt and pepper.

Stuffing and Roasting

1. Remove the thick husks of the chestnuts with a sharp knife. Put the peeled chestnuts in a shallow roasting pan, sprinkle with ¼ cup of water and roast in a preheated 400 °F oven for 8 to 10 minutes, shaking and stirring occasionally, until browned. Let the nuts cool and then using a cloth and small knife, rub and slice off the remaining shell and any dark brown parts. Chop the chestnuts into small pieces.

2. In a frying pan, heat the oil. Add the bacon and fry until crisp. Add the onion and sauté until transparent, stirring occasionally. Transfer the bacon and onion into a bowl and add the chopped chestnuts, bread cubes, chicken broth, eggs, parsley and sage. Stir well and season to taste with salt and pepper.

3. With a spoon, push the stuffing under the loosened breast skin until it is 1 inch thick. Spoon the remaining stuffing into the turkey's cavity. Twist the wings backward and tie the thighs together with kitchen string.

4. Pour some oil onto your hands and rub the turkey to coat it lightly with oil. Put the turkey on a roasting rack set in a roasting pan and roast in a preheated 400 °F oven for 15 minutes. Reduce heat to 325 °F and roast for another 2 hour and 15 minutes, basting the turkey occasionally with the pan juices. Remove when the meat is tender and juices run clear when the thickest section of the thigh meat is pricked with a fork or skewer. Transfer the turkey to a platter and let it rest for 15 minutes before carving. Reserve the pan juices.

Gravy

Set the roasting pan on top of the stove (remove the roasting rack). Add the tomato puree to the pan juices and stir over medium heat for 30 seconds. In a small cup, combine the flour with about ¼ cup of the pan juices and stir or whisk well. Return this to the pan and whisk well to mix. Add 3 cups of water and bring the mixture to a boil. Cook for 5 minutes and then strain the gravy into a separate bowl.

Fried Quince

Cut the quince in half and remove the cores. Brush with melted butter and arrange the quince halves, skin side up, in a single layer in a roasting pan large enough to hold them snugly. Using a small sharp knife, make small crosses in the center of each half and insert a clove in each cross. Sprinkle with confectioners' sugar. Roast in a preheated 350 °F oven for about 25 minutes until tender and a small metal skewer or knife easily penetrate the skin.

Croquettes

Press the uncooked potato croquette dough balls into hedgehog shapes and press slivered almonds into them to create spikes. For the eyes and noses, use peppercorns. Pour enough oil into a pan to reach a depth of 2 or 3 inches and heat over high heat. Deep fry 3 to 5 minutes until brown. Carefully lift from the oil and drain on paper towels. Serve hot.

To Serve

Carve the turkey and serve the stuffing, croquettes and quince on separate plates. Pass the gravy in the gravy boat.

Turkey replaced the goose on the Christmas table in Seventeenth Century England–and became the favorite Christmas dish in Hungary in the following century. This preparation is quite different from the traditional Thanksgiving turkey served in the United States.

Duck, Brézó Style*

4 servings

Duck

Two 4-pound ducks, Salt
½ teaspoon dried marjoram
2 firm apples

Cranberry Apples

4 firm apples
2 tablespoons sugar
2 whole cloves, Juice ½ lemon
½ cup whole cranberry sauce

Side Dish

Two 1-day-old French dinner rolls
(each about 3 ounces)
1 tablespoon vegetable oil
1 slice bacon, chopped
1 tablespoon chopped onion
2 ounces champignon mushrooms, diced
2 ounces dry-smoked sausage, diced
1 tablespoon finely chopped fresh parsley
Salt and freshly ground white pepper
2 large eggs
1 tablespoon unsalted butter
1 tablespoon dried bread crumbs

* Brézói kacsa Mikszáth módra

Duck

1. Sprinkle the ducks inside and out with salt and then sprinkle the marjoram into the cavities.

2. Press a whole apple into each cavity. Place the ducks in a roasting pan and roast in a preheated 325 °F oven for 1 hour and 40 minutes. Baste the ducks occasionally with the pan juices. Turn the ducks once or twice during cooking until golden brown on both sides. If too much fat accumulates in the pan during cooking, pour it off and discard.

4. Remove the ducks from oven but do not turn off the oven. Cut the roasted ducks into quarters and bone them, leaving the breasts and thighs intact. Pour the pan juices into a bowl and set aside. Wipe the pan with a paper towel. Return the duck meat, skin side down, to the roasting pan and roast for about 8 minutes until the skin turns crispy.

Cranberry Apple

1. Trim the stem end from the apples and reserve. Cut a thin slice from the bottom of each apple so that they sit upright. Peel and core the apples. Remove the middle cautiously so as not to puncture the bottom while making enough room for 2 teaspoons of cranberry sauce.

2. In a large saucepan, bring 1 quart of water to a boil. Add the sugar, cloves and lemon juice and then the apples and reserved stem ends. Cook for 3 or 4 minutes; the apples should not be thoroughly cooked. Drain.

3. Fill the apple cavities with cranberry sauce and top with the stem ends. This is best made 30 minutes before serving.

Side Dish

1. Soak the rolls in 2 cups of water until soft. Squeeze out the water and transfer the rolls in a 2-quart saucepan.

2. In a small frying pan, heat the oil and fry the bacon until brown but not crisp. Add the onion and sauté until golden brown. Add the mushrooms and sausage and sauté for 2 or 3 minutes on medium heat. Pour this mixture over the rolls, stirring to mix. Add the parsley, season with salt and pepper and stir in the eggs

3. Butter 4 popover tins or muffin cups and sprinkle with bread crumbs. Press half a roll and a quarter of the mushroom-sausage mixture into the tins and bake for 30 minutes in a preheated 300 °F oven.

To Serve

1. Remove the rolls from the popover tins and put on 4 separate plates. Set 1 apple near each roll. Arrange a duck breast and thigh on each plate and serve.

Crown of Rack of Rabbit
on a Bed of Sausage Lecsó*

4 servings

Potato Side Dish

3 potatoes, peeled
Salt
¼ cup unsalted butter, melted
2 teaspoons finely chopped fresh parsley

Crown Rack of Rabbit

Four ½-pound racks of rabbit,
trimmed, rib bones only
1 tablespoon freshly chopped dried rosemary

* Frissen sült házinyúlkorona kolbászos lecsóval

Salt and freshly ground white pepper
3 tablespoons vegetable oil, for frying

Lecsó

1 tablespoon vegetable oil
2 slices bacon, chopped into small pieces
2 onions, finely chopped
2 teaspoons sweet Hungarian paprika
2 tomatoes, peeled, seeded and diced
6 green bell peppers, diced
4 ounces dry smoked sausage, diced
1 small hot cherry pepper, halved
Salt

Potato Side Dish

Cut the peeled potatoes into quarters and then slice into half-moon shapes. Cook in a saucepan filled with lightly salted water for about 20 minutes until tender. Drain, toss with melted butter and sprinkle with parsley.

Crown Rack of Rabbit

1. Meanwhile, season the rabbit with rosemary, salt and pepper and form each rack into a crown, fastening with a small metal skewer. (See photo on page 95.)

2. In a roasting pan, heat the oil and quickly sear the rabbit crowns on all sides to seal and brown lightly. Arrange the crowns upright in the roasting pan and roast in a preheated 350 °F oven for 10 minutes until cooked. Do not over cook. Set aside and keep warm.

Lecsó

Heat the oil in a frying pan and fry the bacon until browned but not crisp. Add the onions and sauté until golden brown. Remove from heat, stir in the paprika and mix well. Add the tomatoes, peppers, sausage and cherry pepper and season with salt. Return to the heat and simmer, covered, for 8 to 10 minutes.

To Serve

Divide the lecsó among 4 heated plates. Arrange the potatoes around the lecsó to form a wreath. Remove the skewers from the rabbit crowns and place on the lecsó.

I created this dish in honor of a celebrated French chef during his visit to Budapest in 1996. He inspired me to transform a forgotten specialty by emphasizing the character of each ingredient and "crowning" the lecsó with the humble rabbit.

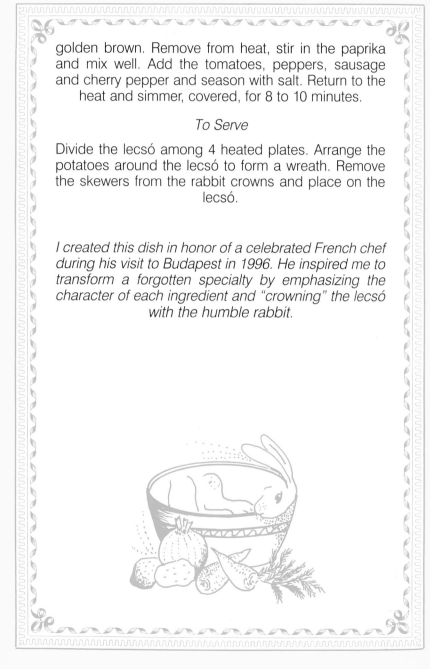

Braided Veal,
Queen Elizabeth Style*

4 servings

Waffle Potatoes

4 potatoes, peeled
Vegetable oil

Stuffed Morels

4 large morel mushrooms
2 ounces goose liver, diced
Salt and freshly ground white pepper
1 tablespoon unsalted butter

* Fonott borjúszűz Erzsébet királynő módra

Potato Puree

1 potato, peeled and quartered, Salt
1 large egg yolk, Grated fresh nutmeg

Gravy

1 cup red wine, such as Gundel Egri Merlot
1 cup Demi-Glace Sauce (see page 182.)

Braided Veal

2 veal tenderloins, trimmed (1¾ pounds total)
3 tablespoons mixed chopped fresh herbs,
such as rosemary, sage, oregano, or basil
Salt, 3 tablespoons vegetable oil
Wild Rice Confetti (see page 188.)

Garnish

Fresh rosemary, sage, or basil, for garnish

Waffle Potatoes

1. One or 2 hours before serving, slice the peeled potatoes with a mandoline, cutting across the width of the potato to make round, waffle-patterned slices. You will need 5 slices from each potato, but it is a good idea to cut the potatoes so that there are a few extra.

2. Pour the vegetable oil into a heavy pot or deep-fat fryer to a depth of 2 or 3 inches and heat until very hot. Deep fry the waffle potatoes until golden brown and crispy. Drain on paper towels and set aside.

Stuffed Morels

1. Blanch the morels in boiling water for a few seconds. Drain and dry with a soft cloth or paper towel.

2. Sprinkle the goose liver with salt and pepper and spoon it equally into the morel cavities. Melt the butter in a small frying pan over low heat. Add the morels, season with salt and pepper and cook, shaking the pan gently, for about 2 minutes. Set aside until ready to serve. (These can be prepared up to 30 minutes in advance.)

Potato Puree

In a saucepan of lightly salted boiling water, cook the potatoes for about 15 minutes until tender. Drain and transfer to a bowl. Using a potato masher or fork, mash the potatoes. Add the egg yolk and mash until smooth. Season with nutmeg and salt, cover and set aside to keep warm.

Gravy

Boil the wine over medium-high heat until reduced by three-quarters. Add the demi-glace, return to the boil and then remove from the heat. Stir well, cover and keep warm.

Braided Veal

1. Cut the veal tenderloins in half lengthwise and then cut each into 3 strips, leaving them attached at one end. This is to prepare the meat for braiding. Sprinkle the strips with herbs and salt.

2. Weave each piece into a braid to make 4 braids. Lightly oil the outside of a 10-by-2-inch steel tube (such as a cake pan). Wrap 1 braid around the outside of the tube and fasten the ends with a metal skewer or toothpick. (See photo.)

3. Heat the oil on a griddle or in a large frying pan. Sauté the veal braid for about 7 minutes, rolling it to brown the meat evenly. Carefully pull the meat from the

tube and set aside to keep warm. Repeat with the remaining veal braids, cooking them one at a time. Rub the tube with oil as needed and add more oil to the griddle as needed.

To Serve

1. Place 1 fried veal braid in the middle of a plate, fill it with Wild Rice Confetti and set a stuffed morel on top of the rice.

2. Spoon the potato puree into a pastry bag fitted with a star tip and press 5 stars around the top of each veal crown. Insert a waffle potato in these stars.

3. Brush the sides of the meat with the gravy and garnish with fresh herbs.

In May 1993, Gundel was privileged to arrange the State Luncheon in honor of Her Majesty Queen Elizabeth II when she and Philip the Duke of Edinburgh visited Hungary. It was the first time an English monarch had visited Hungary and I created this dish for the festive event. George Lang suggested that every dish on the menu be made in the shape of a crown.

Veal Chops, Pittsburgh Style*

4 servings

Veal Chops

Four ½-pound veal chops
9 ounces goose liver, cut into 4 slices
Salt and freshly ground white pepper
3 tablespoons vegetable oil

Potato Baskets

4 potatoes, peeled, Vegetable oil

Sauce

1 tablespoon vegetable oil
4 champignon mushrooms, chopped

* Borjúborda Pittsburgh-i módra

2 ounces boiled ham,
thinly slices into strips
1 cup Brown Sauce (see page 181.)
½ cup dry red wine
Salt and freshly ground white pepper

Corn with Cream

¼ cup unsalted butter
2 cups fresh or frozen,
defrosted corn kernels
1 tablespoon all-purpose flour
2 tablespoons finely chopped fresh dill
Salt
1 cup heavy cream
4 servings Potato Croquettes
(see page 189.)

Veal Chops

1. Sprinkle the chops and goose liver slices with salt and pepper, cover and refrigerate for at least 1 hour.

2. In a large frying pan, heat 2 tablespoons of oil over high heat. Add the chops and sauté until browned on both sides. Transfer to a roasting pan and roast in a pre-heated 350 °F oven for about 15 minutes, until cooked.

3. In a frying pan, heat 1 tablespoon of oil over medium-high heat and sauté the goose livers for 2 minutes on each side. Drain on paper towels, patting the liver slices to remove as much oil as possible.

Potato Baskets

1. About 1 hour before serving, slice the peeled potatoes with a mandoline, cutting across the width of the

potato to make round, waffle-patterned slices. You will need 5 slices from each potato, but it is a good idea to cut the potatoes so that there are a few extra.

2. Arrange 5 potato slices in a small basket designed for making deep-fried potato baskets, placing them to make a basket. Set the smaller basket on top of the potatoes to hold the basket shape. Heat the oil until very hot and deep fry the potato basket until crisp. Drain and set aside. Repeat with the remaining potatoes to make 4 baskets. (This can be done 1 hour ahead of time.)

Sauce

1. In a frying pan, heat the oil over medium-high heat. Add the mushrooms and ham and sauté for 3 minutes.

2. Add the Brown Sauce and wine and boil until reduced by two-thirds. Season with salt and pepper, cover and set aside to keep warm.

Corn with Cream

In a 2-quart saucepan, melt the butter over medium heat. Add the corn and cook, stirring, for about 4 minutes. Sprinkle with flour and stir with a wooden spoon. Add the dill and cream, season with salt, stir well and bring to a boil. Reduce the heat and simmer for 3 or 4 minutes, stirring occasionally. Remove from the heat, cover and keep warm.

To Serve

1. Spoon some creamed corn over a third of each plate (you will not use all the creamed corn). Pool 2 tablespoons of the sauce on another third of the

place. Set a chop of top of the sauce and a slice of liver on top of the chop.

2. Put the potato baskets in the remaining third of the plates and fill them with the croquettes.

3. Serve the remaining corn and sauce separately.

Károly Gundel created this dish to honor the mayor of Pittsburgh when he visited Budapest in 1930.

Stuffed Kohlrabies*

4 servings

8 young kohlrabis, leaves attached
1 bunch fresh parsley
One 1-day-old French dinner roll (about 3 ounces)
1 cup heavy cream
1 pound ground veal
1 large egg
Salt and freshly ground white pepper
1 cup chicken broth
1 tablespoon unsalted butter
3 tablespoons all-purpose flour
1 cup milk

* Töltött karalábé

1. Trim the kohlrabi leaves from the bulb, leaving the 2 or 3 smallest leaves attached. slice the stem end of the kohlrabis, with the small leaves attached, to make lids. Set the lids aside.

2. Reserve the 4 largest leaves. Chop the remaining kohlrabi leaves with the parsley.

3. Scald the 4 reserved leaves in boiling water for 30 seconds. Drain immediately and lay flat on a work surface.

4. Peel the kohlrabi bulbs and, using a melon baller, scoop out the flesh to make shells. Set the flesh and bulbs aside.

5. In a large bowl, soak the roll in ½ cup of the cream. Add the veal, egg, half the parsley-kohlrabi mixture and season with salt and pepper and mix well, breaking up the roll. Spoon the filling into the kohlrabi shells and then divide the remaining filling among the 4 scalded leaves. Roll the leaves into secure packages.

6. Put the stuffed kohlrabis, stuffed leaves, the reserved kohlrabi flesh and the remaining parsley-kohlrabi mixture in a large saucepan. Add the chicken broth and 1 cup of water. Cover and simmer until the kohlrabi bulbs are tender. Transfer the kohlrabi bulbs and stuffed leaves to a bowl, cover and keep warm.

7. In a frying pan, melt the butter over medium heat. Add the flour and stir with a wooden spoon until well mixed. Remove from the heat and whisk in the milk and remaining ½ cup of cream until smooth. Pour this mixture into the kohlrabi cooking liquid. Bring to a boil, reduce the heat to low and cook for 10 minutes, stirring continuously. Season with salt, if necessary.

To Serve

1. In a saucepan, bring 2 cups of water to a boil and

scald the reserved kohlrabi lids for about 3 minutes. Drain.

2. Pour the sauce over the stuffed kohlrabis and leaves. Set the lids on the bulbs and serve.

Kohlrabi is the sweetest member of the turnip family, and also is known as cabbage turnip. It is available from mid-spring to mid-autumn. This dish was created for a wine-tasting dinner in Gundel's Susanna Lorántffy wine cellar, located on the lower level of the restaurant.

Veal Stew, Pörkölt Style, with Egg Dumplings*

4 servings

¼ cup vegetable oil
2 onions, finely chopped
1 small clove garlic, crushed
2 tablespoons sweet Hungarian paprika
1¾ pounds veal shoulder or thigh,
cut into 1-inch cubes
Salt
2 yellow bell peppers, diced
1 tomato, peeled, seeded and diced
Hot Hungarian paprika
½ cup diced green, red or yellow bell peppers
4 servings Egg Dumplings (see page 187.)

* Borjúpörkölt galuskával

1. In a medium-size pan, heat all but 1 teaspoon of the oil and sauté the onions until golden brown. Remove from the heat and stir in garlic and sweet paprika. Add ¾ cup of water and the veal. Bring to a boil over high heat. Reduce the heat, season to taste with salt, cover and simmer for 20 to 25 minutes, until the meat is nearly cooked through.

2. Add the yellow peppers, tomato, and hot paprika and simmer for about 8 minutes until the vegetables are tender. (Serve immediately or make this ahead of time and reheat slowly over low heat.)

To Serve

1. Heat the remaining teaspoon of oil in a frying pan and sauté the diced peppers for about 3 minutes.

2. Divide the hot dumplings among four warm plates. Make a well in the center of the dumplings and ladle the veal stew and gravy into it. Garnish with the diced peppers.

Tenderloin Steak
à la Franz Liszt*

4 servings

1¾ pounds tenderloin of beef,
cut into 4 fillet mignons
Salt and freshly ground white pepper
½ cup vegetable oil
10 ounces goose liver, cut into 4 slices
4 servings Potato Croquettes (see page 189.)
4 champignon mushroom caps
4 servings Wild Mushroom Sauce with Red Wine
(see page 183.)
Fresh vegetables of your choice

** Bélszínjava Liszt Ferenc módján libamájjal
és Egri Merlot borral készült vadgombamártással*

1. Shape the tenderloin slices into round fillets and season with salt and pepper. Tie each around the circumference with kitchen string to maintain its shape.

2. In an oven-proof frying pan, heat ¼ cup of the oil over medium-high heat. Add the fillets and sauté for about 2 minutes, turning once, until rose colored. Put the pan in a preheated 350 °F oven until done to your satisfaction. For rare, roast for 8 minutes; for medium-rare, roast for 12 minutes; for well done, roast for 18 minutes.

3. Season the goose liver slices with salt and pepper. In a separate frying pan, heat 1 tablespoon of oil over low heat. Add the goose liver slices and sauté for about 2 minutes. Turn over and sauté for 1 minute longer. Remove from the pan and set aside, covered, to keep warm. Wipe the pan with a paper towel.

4. Cut a thin slice off the top of each mushroom cap and cut a pattern into the caps, if desired. In the frying pan used for the goose liver, heat the remaining 3 tablespoons of oil over medium heat. Add the mushrooms and cook for about 3 minutes, stirring occasionally.

To Serve

1. Cut off the string from the fillet mignons and discard. Set a fillet in the center of each plate and lay a slice of goose liver on top of it. Garnish with the mushrooms.

2. Circle the meat with vegetables and potato croquettes. Serve the Wild Mushroom Sauce with red wine separately.

The inspiration for this superb dish is Tournedos à la Rossini, in which the composer combined the heart of the beef fillet with foie gras, truffles and Madeira sauce. We named our recipe after the great Hungarian composer, Franz Liszt, who we are sure would have loved our variation.

Tenderloin
of Beef Habsburg*

4 servings

Pastry
1 pound commercial frozen puff pastry,
defrosted
1 large egg, lightly beaten
4 ounces dried beans or pie weights

Stew
3 ounces sweetbreads, cubed
3 or 4 cocks combs, optional
1 teaspoon salt, 2 tablespoons unsalted butter
1 small onion, diced
3 ounces boletus mushrooms,
cut into 1-inch cubes
1 bunch fresh parsley, chopped

* Bélszínszeletek Habsburg-menyegző módra

Salt and freshly ground white pepper
1 cup Demi-Glace Sauce (see page 182.)

Side Dishes

4 green Savoy cabbage leaves,
each about the size of your palm
Salt, Pinch of baking soda
4 servings Wild Rice Confetti (see page 188.)
8 baby carrots,
boiled for 8 minutes and drained
1 tablespoon unsalted butter

Tenderloin

1¾ pounds tenderloin of beef,
cut into 8 fillet mignons
Salt and freshly ground white pepper
¼ cup vegetable oil

Pastry

1. On a lightly floured work surface, roll out half the puff pastry until very thin. Cut four 4-inch-diameter circles from the pastry. Reserve the remaining pastry.

2. Line four round baking molds, each 2 inches in diameter and ½ inch deep, with the pastry circles, letting the sides ride up the sides. These will become the pastry pans. Cut 4 strips, no wider than your finger, from the remaining pastry. Attach to the inside of the pastry pans to form handles, securing them with beaten egg and supporting them with foil. (See photo.) Fill the pastry pans with dried beans or pastry weights. Set the baking molds on a baking sheet or in a baking pan and bake in a preheated 350 °F oven for 10 minutes.

3. Roll out the other half of the puffed pastry and cut four 2-inch circles to act as lids. Place a small button, made of pastry, in the center of each lid. Brush with

beaten egg, lay on an ungreased baking sheet and bake for 8 minutes in a preheated 350 °F oven.

4. Remove pastry pans from the oven and pour out the beans. Pair the pastry pans with lids and set aside.

Stew

1. In a 2-quart saucepan, bring a quart of water to a boil over high heat. Add the sweetbreads, cocks combs, if using, and salt. Reduce the heat and simmer for 15 minutes. Drain and set the sweetbreads aside. Cut the cocks combs into 1 inch pieces, if using.

2. Melt the butter in a 2-quart saucepan and sauté the onion until golden brown. Add the mushrooms and sauté for 2 minutes longer. Add the sweetbreads and cocks combs, sprinkle with parsley, season with salt and pepper and then pour the demi-glace sauce over all. Bring to a boil, reduce the heat and simmer for 5 minutes. Set aside to keep warm.

Side Dishes

1. In a 2 quart saucepan, bring 1 quart of salted water to a boil. Stir in the baking soda and return to the boil. Stir the Savoy cabbage leaves into the water and cook for 2 minutes. Drain and rinse with cold water.

2. Lay 1 leaf on a piece of cheesecloth and spoon some Wild Rice Confetti in the center of each leaf (you will not use all the rice). Fold the leaf into a ball and roll up in the cheesecloth. Transfer to a roasting pan and brush with melted butter. Cover with foil and keep warm in a preheated 300 °F oven.

3. In a small frying pan, melt the butter over medium heat. Add the carrots and sauté for 2 minutes. Transfer to the roasting pan with the Savoy balls, cover and keep warm in the oven.

Tenderloin

1. Shape the tenderloin slices into rounds and season with salt and pepper.

2. In an oven-proof frying pan, heat the oil over medium-high heat. Add the fillets and sauté for about 2 minutes, turning once, until rose colored. Put the pan in a preheated 350 °F oven until done to your satisfaction. For rare, roast for 4 minutes; for medium-rare, roast for 6 minutes; for well done, roast for 9 minutes.

To Serve

1. Unwrap the cabbage balls. Put the cabbage balls and the carrots on each of 4 plates. Set a puff pastry pan near the vegetables and fill the pans with stew. Set the lids on the stew.

2. Lay the tenderloins on the front of the plates. Serve the remaining stew and wild rice separately.

I created this dish on the occasion of the marriage of Princess Walburga Habsburg and Count Archibald Douglas in the summer of 1996. It was served for their wedding dinner.

Tycoon's Goulash*

4 servings

Sauce

3 tablespoons vegetable oil
1 cup finely chopped onion
2 cloves garlic, crushed
2 tablespoons sweet Hungarian paprika
½ teaspoon ground caraway seeds
1½ pounds veal bone, cut into 2-inch pieces
(the bone must not be splintery)
Salt
1 tomato, peeled, seeded and diced
1 yellow bell pepper, diced
1 small hot cherry pepper,
seeded and chopped, optional

Meat

3 tablespoons vegetable oil
1¾ pounds tenderloin of beef,
cut into 1 inch cubes
Salt
Little Pinched Noodles (see page 186.)

Sauce

1. In a frying pan, heat the oil over medium-high heat. Add the onion and garlic and sauté for about 10 minutes until golden brown.

* Mágnásgulyás

2. Remove the pan from the heat. Stir in the sweet paprika, caraway seeds and 3 cups of water. Add the veal bones and season with salt. Cook for 1 hour over low heat. Replace the water that evaporates, so that you up with 2 cups of sauce.

3. Remove the bones, add the tomato, peppers and cherry pepper and simmer for 15 minutes. If the sauce is too thin, increase the heat to medium and cook for a few minutes until thickened. Transfer the sauce to a smaller pan, cover and set aside to keep warm.

Meat

In a large frying pan, heat the oil over medium-high heat. Add the meat, season lightly with salt and cook, stirring, for 4 or 5 minutes until browned but still pink on the inside. (You may have to use 2 pans or cook the meat in batches. Do not crowd the pan.)

To Serve

Put the meat on warm plates and pour the sauce over it. Top with noodles and serve immediately.

Goulash is one of the most varied recipes of the Hungarian kitchen. Indicative of its international fame, is that there are 27 varieties of the dish in the Sacher cookbook, published in Vienna, Austria.

Tycoon's Goulash has its origins in Hungary, although no one knows who created it, or when. In our version, instead of stewing the beef, I sauté it briefly. This way the meat is tender and juicy and remains pink inside.

Gundel Ragout, Tokány Style*

4 servings

Sauce

2 tablespoons unsalted butter
2 tablespoons chopped onions
½ pound button mushrooms, sliced
1 heaped tablespoon chopped fresh parsley
Salt and freshly ground white pepper
1 cup red wine, such as Gundel Egri Merlot
1½ cups Brown Sauce (see page 181.)

Vegetables

4 ounces white asparagus,
cut into 1½ inch lengths

* Gundel-tokány

3 ounces green beans,
cut into 1½ inch lengths
Pinch of baking soda

Meat

1¾ pounds beef tenderloin,
about ¾ inch thick,
trimmed and cut into 2-inch-long strips
½ pound goose liver, cut into 4 slices
5 tablespoons vegetable oil
Salt and freshly ground white pepper
4 servings Potato Croquettes
(see page 189.)

Sauce

1. In a 10-inch frying pan, melt the butter. Add the onions and sauté until transparent. Cook for about 3 minutes or longer until tender. Add the mushrooms and sauté for 3 minutes longer. Season with parsley, salt and pepper.

2. In a saucepan, bring the red wine to a boil and cook for 10 to 15 minutes until reduced to 2 tablespoons. Add to the onion-mushroom mixture. Add the brown sauce, stir and simmer for 5 minutes. Cover and set aside to keep warm.

Vegetables

Cook the asparagus and the green beans separately in lightly salted water for about 10 minutes each. Add a pinch of baking soda to the cooking water for the green beans. Cover and set aside. Reheat in the cooking water just before serving.

Meat

1. Sprinkle the goose liver lightly with salt. In a small frying pan, heat 1 tablespoon of oil and fry for 2 minutes on each side. Remove from the pan, cover and set aside to keep warm.

2. In a separate frying pan, heat the remaining 4 tablespoons of oil over high heat. Add the tenderloin strips, season with salt and pepper, and sauté for about 6 minutes, turning the meat several times, until cooked. (You may have to use 2 pans or cook the meat in batches. Do not crowd the pan.)

3. Stir the meat into the hot mushroom sauce.

To Serve

Serve the meat with plenty of sauce. Garnish each plate with asparagus and green beans. Arrange the potato croquettes in a circle around the meat and lay a slice of goose liver on top of each serving of meat.

Pan-Fried Lamb Chops
on Cabbage Pancakes
with Crisp Vegetable Straws*

4 servings

Pancakes

1 pound cabbage
1 tablespoon salt plus a pinch
1 tablespoon granulated sugar
¼ cup vegetable oil
Freshly ground white pepper
½ cup all-purpose flour
1 large egg
¾ cup milk

** Rózsaszínűre sütött báránykaraj
káposztás palacsintán, ropogós zöldségszalmával*

Vegetable Straw

2 tablespoons vegetable oil
1 cup julienne carrots
1 cup julienne celery
1 cup julienne leek
1 cup julienne zucchini
1½ teaspoons soy sauce

Lamb

2 pounds loin lamb chops
1 tablespoon minced fresh thyme
1 tablespoon minced fresh rosemary
Salt and freshly ground white pepper
2 tablespoons vegetable oil
4 servings Garlic Compote,
optional (see page 185.)

Pancakes

1. Shred the cabbage, put it in a bowl, sprinkle with 1 tablespoon of salt, toss well and set aside for 30 minutes. Using your hands, squeeze the liquid from the cabbage.

2. In a large, deep frying pan, heat the sugar over medium heat until it liquefies. Add 2 tablespoons of oil and the cabbage and simmer for 15 minutes, stirring continuously. Season with pepper, stir and remove from the heat. Set aside to cool.

3. In a 1-quart saucepan, combine the flour, egg, milk and pinch of salt and stir until smooth. If mixture is too thick, add a little mineral water; if it is too thin, add a little flour. Stir in the cooled cabbage and mix well to make a batter.

4. Heat a 6-inch frying pan lightly coated with oil over medium-high heat. Add enough pancake batter to cover the bottom of the pan and cook for about 2 minutes. Turn the pancake and cook for about 1 minute longer until lightly browned on both sides. Transfer the pancake to a plate and cover to keep warm. Repeat with the remaining batter to make 4 pancakes.

Vegetable Straw

In a 10-inch frying pan, heat the oil over high heat. Add the carrots and celery and sauté for 1½ minutes. Add the leeks and zucchini and sauté for about 1½ minutes longer until crisp-tender. Sprinkle with soy sauce.

Lamb

1. Season the lamb chops with thyme, rosemary and salt and pepper.

2. In a large oven-proof frying pan, heat the oil over medium-high heat. Add the lamb chops and sauté lamb for 4 minutes on each side. Roast in a preheated 350 °F oven for 12 to 15 minutes until browned on the outside and pink in the center. Do not overcook

To Serve

Place a pancake on each of 4 warm plates. Cover half of the pancake with vegetable straw. Cut the pancake from the center to the rim and fold a quarter over the vegetables (see photo). Cut the lamb into slices and arrange the slices next to the pancakes. Serve hot with Garlic Compote, if desired. (I recommend it for garlic fans.)

Many years ago, I presented this dish to Dr. Gábor Buday, at the time the general manager of the Hotel Forum and now the CEO of Gundel. Ever since, it has been his favorite.

Grilled Pork with Wild Mushroom Stew and Cottage Cheese Noodles*

4 servings

Pork

1¾ pounds pork tenderloin
(4 small tenderloins or 2 large ones)
1 tablespoon finely chopped fresh thyme
Salt and freshly ground white pepper
3 tablespoons vegetable oil

Cottage Cheese Noodles

1½ cups cottage cheese
2 large eggs

* Grillezett sertéscopf vadgombapörkölttel, túrós galuskával

⅓ cup semolina flour

1 tablespoon unsalted butter, softened

Salt

Mushroom Stew

3 tablespoons vegetable oil

1 onion, finely chopped

2 teaspoons sweet Hungarian paprika

1 tomato, peeled,
seeded and finely chopped

1 pound mushrooms, chopped

Salt

Pork

One hour before cooking, cut the pork tenderloins lengthwise into 3 strips each, leaving them attached at one end. Season with thyme, salt and pepper. Fasten the ends with small metal skewers or toothpicks. In a deep oven-proof skillet, heat the oil over medium-high heat. Cook the meat for 3 minutes on each side until lightly browned. Roast in a preheated 325 °F oven for 10 to 12 minutes.

Cottage Cheese Noodles

In a bowl, combine the cottage cheese, eggs, flour and butter and season with salt. Stir well, cover and refrigerate for 30 minutes. Using a spoon, form the dough into noodle shapes and drop the noodles into lightly salted boiling water. Lower the heat, cover and simmer for about 12 minutes until the noodles rise to the surface. Drain and rinse briefly in cool water.

Mushroom Stew

In a 1-quart saucepan, heat the oil over medium-high heat. Add the onions and sauté until golden brown. Remove from the heat, stir in the paprika, tomato and ½ cup of water. Return to the heat and simmer until the tomato is tender and nearly all the water has evaporated. Add the mushrooms and season with salt. Cover and simmer for a few minutes until the mushrooms are tender.

To Serve

Spoon the mushroom stew on plates. Separate the pork into strips and set on top of the stew. Spoon the noodles around the stew.

Pork Tenderloin Stuffed with Prunes and Sautéed with Hazelnuts*

4 servings

Pears
4 half-ripe pears, 2 cups red wine
3 tablespoons granulated sugar

Filling
4 ounces pitted prunes
½ teaspoon coriander seeds
1 bay leaf, 1 firm apple
1 large egg, 2 tablespoons bread crumbs

Pork
1¾ pounds pork tenderloin, trimmed (2 tenderloins)
Salt

* Aszalt szilvával töltött sertésszűz mogyoróval sütve

3 ounces hazelnuts, coarsely chopped
2 tablespoons vegetable oil

Sauce

2 tablespoons unsalted butter
½ cup Brown Sauce (see page 181.)
2 tablespoons orange juice, ½ cup heavy cream
Salt

Pears

1. Peel the pears but leave the stem ends intact. Cut a wavy collar from the skin around the stem ends. Cut a slice from the bottom of the pears and remove the cores.

2. In a saucepan large enough to hold the pears comfortably, bring the wine and sugar to a boil. Set the pears in the wine, return to the boil and cook for 1 or 2 minutes. Remove from the pan and let the pears cool in the cooking liquid.

Filling

1. Rinse the prunes with lukewarm water and transfer to a 1-quart saucepan. Remove 1 cup of the wine cooking liquid from the pears and add to the saucepan with the prunes. Bring to a boil over medium heat. Add the coriander seeds and bay leaf, remove from the heat and set aside.

2. Peel and core the apple and cut into thin slices. Add to the prunes. Stir in the egg and bread crumbs until well mixed.

Pork

1. Using a thin-bladed knife, make "tunnels" lengthwise in the centers of the tenderloins. Insert the filling

into the tunnels, packing it firmly and fastening the ends with small metal skewers, toothpicks or meat needles. Roll the tenderloins in the nuts. Reserve the nuts that do not cling to the meat.

2. In a large frying pan, heat the oil over medium-high heat. Add the meat and cook for about 5 minutes on each side, turning constantly, until the meat turns pink. Roast in a preheated 350 °F oven for about 15 minutes until cooked through.

Sauce

1. Melt the butter in a 1-quart saucepan. Add the remaining hazelnuts and sauté for a few minutes. Add the brown sauce and juice, bring to a boil and cook for 2 or 3 minutes.

2. Add the cream, season with salt and return to the boil. Cook for 3 minutes. Remove from heat, cover and keep warm.

To Serve

1. Remove pears from red wine and drain. Make several slices in each pear nearly to the base and then spread each one into a fan. Place the pear fans on each of 4 warm plates. Spoon a little sauce in the center of the plates.

2. Cut the meat diagonally into slices. Stand 2 slices on each plate. Serve the remaining sauce in a sauce boat.

I hope you will agree with the judges who gave me the Toque d'Or Award for this dish in 1988.

Stuffed Cabbage, Our Way*

4 servings

Filling

1 tablespoon vegetable oil
¼ cup rice
Pinch of salt
2 slices bacon, cut into small pieces
1 onion, finely chopped
8 ounces ground pork shoulder
4 ounces ground beef shoulder
1 large egg
2 teaspoons sweet Hungarian paprika
1 clove garlic, crushed
Pinch of dry marjoram
½ teaspoon freshly ground white pepper
1 small hot cherry pepper,
seeded and chopped, optional
Salt
4 large cabbage leaves
Cider vinegar

Cabbage

2 pounds sauerkraut
1½ pounds smoked pork ribs (4 ribs)
Salt
Freshly ground black pepper

* Töltött káposzta Gundel módra

Hot Hungarian paprika
2 tablespoons vegetable oil
1 tablespoon all-purpose flour, 1 onion, diced
2 teaspoons sweet Hungarian paprika
2 tablespoons chopped fresh dill
1¼ cups sour cream
8 small smoked sausages, as garnish

Filling

1. In a small saucepan, heat the oil over medium heat. Add the rice and sauté until lightly browned. Add ¼ cup of water and simmer until the rice is half cooked. Set aside to cool.

2. Sauté the bacon in a small frying pan until browned. Add the onions and cook until golden. Transfer to a bowl. Add the meat, rice, paprika, garlic, marjoram, pepper and cherry pepper, if using, and season with salt. Stir well.

3. Remove the thick veins from the cabbage leaves. Bring a pot of water to a boil. Add a little vinegar and boil the cabbage leaves until softened. Drain and lay the leaves on a work surface. Divide the ground meat filling among the leaves and fold the leaves over and around the filling to encase it.

Cabbage

1. Rinse the sauerkraut. Put half of it on the bottom of a 10-inch saucepan and lay the cabbage leaves and pork ribs on top. Cover with the remaining sauerkraut. Add enough water to cover the sauerkraut. Cover and simmer for 1½ hours. Season with salt, pepper and hot paprika. Add more water during cooking, if necessary, to keep the sauerkraut from drying out.

2. In a small frying pan, heat the oil. Add the flour and onion and sauté until blended and the onion softens. Remove from heat, stir in the sweet paprika, dill and 1 cup of sour cream. Remove the ribs and stuffed cabbage leaves from the sauerkraut and set aside, covered, to keep warm. Pour the sour cream roux over the sauerkraut, stir gently, and simmer for 10 minutes, stirring occasionally.

To Serve

Spoon the sauerkraut in a warm shallow 10-inch bowl. Top with the stuffed cabbage leaves and ribs. Garnish with the remaining sour cream and the smoked sausages.

I discovered this old Gundel recipe in our archives. Károly Gundel enriched the traditional stuffed cabbage with smoked pork ribs.

Game

Breast of Pheasant, Count Széchenyi Style*

4 servings

Pheasant

2 pounds boneless, skinless pheasant breasts
(4 breasts halves), bones reserved ½ teaspoon salt
¼ teaspoon freshly ground white pepper
¼ teaspoon dried marjoram or 2 level teaspoons
chopped fresh marjoram
8 ounces goose liver, 1 teaspoon cognac
2 ounces trumpet mushrooms
4 slices bacon, 1 tablespoon vegetable oil

Spring Cabbage

Pheasant bones (reserved from the breasts)
Salt, 2 pounds Savoy cabbage leaves
3 slices bacon, sliced into strips

* Fácánmell gróf Széchenyi módra

1 tablespoon heavy cream
¼ teaspoon dried marjoram or 2 level teaspoons
chopped fresh marjoram
¼ teaspoon freshly ground white pepper

Apples

2 tablespoons unsalted butter
4 small, firm apples, peeled, cored and sliced

Pheasant

1. Split the breasts halves, spread open and sprinkle with salt, pepper and marjoram. Cut the goose liver into 8 slices and sprinkle with salt and cognac.

2. Put the mushrooms in a mesh strainer and submerge in boiling water for 3 minutes to scald. Lift from the water and drain.

3. Divide the mushrooms equally among the liver slices to make 4 sandwiches. Set 1 sandwich on each split breast and fold the meat over to encase the liver.

4. Wrap the bacon around the stuffed breasts and secure with toothpicks. In a frying pan, heat the oil over medium-high heat. Add the bacon-wrapped breasts and brown for about 2 minutes on each side. Transfer to a baking pan and roast in a preheated 350 °F oven for 12 minutes until cooked through. Remove the toothpicks but leave the bacon around the pheasant breasts.

Spring Cabbage

1. Put the pheasant bones in a small roasting pan and roast in a preheated 350 °F oven for 20 minutes to brown. Transfer the bones to a 2-quart saucepan, add 1 quart of water and bring to a boil over high heat. Reduce the heat and simmer for 2 hours until the liquid

reduces to ½ cup. Strain the liquid and season to taste with salt. Discard the bones.

2. Cut the cabbage leaves into ½-inch strips. Set in a small strainer (the one used for the mushrooms is fine) and immerse in boiling water for 3 minutes to scald. Lift from the water and drain.

3. Fry the bacon in a dry frying pan until brown but not crisp. Drain.

4. In a bowl, combine the cabbage and bacon. Add the cream, 1 tablespoon of pheasant essence, marjoram and pepper. Bring to a boil, reduce the heat to medium and cook for 3 minutes.

Apples

Melt the butter in a large frying pan. Add the apple slices and cook, stirring and turning constantly, for about 4 minutes.

To Serve

Spoon the cabbage-bacon mixture on one side of each plate. Lay a pheasant breast in the center of each plate and surround them with apples. Spoon a little of the pheasant essence over the pheasant and serve the remaining separately.

Count Stephen Széchenyi was a passionate hunter when he was young. He had a great kitchen with some of the most famous chefs of the day. Luckily for us, several of the chefs have kept a record of the dishes that were cooked at dinners served at Széchenyi Castle in Nagycenk, western Hungary includin the one above.

Venison
Two Ways*

4 servings

Braised Venison Leg

1 pound boneless venison leg
Salt
4 juniper berries, crushed
4 black peppercorns
1 tablespoon vegetable oil
1 carrot, peeled and sliced
1 parsnip, peeled and sliced

** Grillezett őzérem és Gundel Egri Merlot-jával
párolt őzcomb tökpürével
és gesztenyés burgonyáskosárral*

1 stalk celery, sliced
1 onion, sliced
1 teaspoon tomato paste
½ cup dry red wine,
such as Gundel Egri Merlot
3 cups Veal Stock (see page 179.)
2 teaspoons potato starch

Potato Nest

2 baking potatoes, peeled and julienned
Vegetable oil

Pureed Pumpkin

8 ounces pumpkin, quartered
and seeds removed
1 large potato,
peeled and cut into 2 inch pieces
1 tablespoon unsalted butter, softened
Salt

Chestnuts

1 teaspoon granulated sugar
2 tablespoons unsalted butter
24 fresh chestnuts, peeled

Venison Medallions

1 pound boneless venison loin
Salt and freshly ground black pepper
4 juniper berries, crushed
2 tablespoons vegetable oil

Braised Venison Leg

1. Lightly sprinkle the leg with salt and press the
berries and peppercorns into the meat.

2. In a large, deep frying pan, heat the oil over high heat. Cook the leg for 8 to 10 minutes on each side until well browned. Remove from the pan and set aside. Add the carrot, parsnip and celery to the same pan and cook, stirring constantly, for 3 minutes. Add the onion and cook, stirring, for 3 minutes longer until the vegetables are soft but not mushy. Add the tomato paste and the red wine and stir well.

3. Return the meat to the pan, add the veal stock and season with salt. Bring to a boil, reduce the heat, cover and simmer until the meat softens. (Depending on the quality of the meat, this can take as long as 2 hours; begin checking after 1 hour.) Add water to the pan as the stock evaporates to keep the meat from drying out. When the meat is tender, lift it from the pan and set aside, covered, to keep warm.

4. Bring the sauce in the pan to a boil. Stir the potato starch with 1 teaspoon of water, add this slurry to the boiling sauce and boil for 4 or 5 minutes. Strain the sauce through a very fine filter (such as a coffee filter or tea strainer). Cut the leg meat into 4 pieces and return it to the strained sauce, cover and set aside. Just before serving, reheat slowly.

Potato Nests

Put a quarter of the julienned potatoes in a small basket designed for making deep-fried potato baskets. Set the smaller basket on top of the potatoes to hold the basket shape. Heat the oil until very hot and deep fry the potato basket until crisp. Drain and set aside. Repeat with the remaining potatoes to make 4 baskets. (This can be done 1 hour ahead of time.)

Pureed Pumpkin

1. Roast the pumpkin in a preheated 350 °F oven for 20

minutes. Scrape the flesh from the shell and transfer to a food processor and puree until smooth.

2. Boil the potatoes in salted water for about 15 minutes until tender, about 15 minutes. Add to the pumpkin puree and process just until mixed. Add the butter and salt and mix well. Cover to keep warm.

Chestnuts

In a dry 2-quart saucepan, cook the sugar over high heat until it turns light brown. Add 3 tablespoons of water and bring to a boil. Stir until the sugar melts. Reduce the heat, add the butter and chestnuts and simmer for 2 minutes, tossing to coat the nuts with the butter.

Medallions

1. Cut the venison into 4 thick slices. Shape into round medallions, season with salt and pepper and press juniper berries into the top of each Tie each around the circumference with kitchen string to maintain its shape.

2. In a frying pan, heat the oil and cook the medallions for 1 or 2 minutes on each side.

To Serve

1. Put pureed pumpkin in a pastry bag fitted with a rose tip. Make 2 roses on each plate. Fill the potato nests with the caramelized chestnuts and place them between the roses.

2. Put 1 piece of leg meat on each plate in front of the potato nests and drizzle with the sauce. Remove the string from each one and put a medallion on top of the leg meat.

I invented this festive game dish for the reopening of Gundel in 1992.

Veal-Stuffed
Roasted Sirloin of Venison
in Sesame Crust*

4 servings

Sauce

1 cup Demi-Glace Sauce (see page 182.),
made with venison bones
½ cup red wine, Gundel Egri Merlot
Salt

Potatoes

3 large potatoes, peeled
1 tablespoon unsalted butter

**** Rózsaszínűre sült szarvashátszín borjúszűzzel töltve
szezámmagos bundában, Gundel Egri Merlot mártással,
zöldségekkel és lerakott burgonyával***

1 teaspoon chopped fresh thyme
1 cup heavy cream

Veal Tenderloin and Venison Sirloin

5 ounces veal tenderloin, trimmed
Salt and freshly ground white pepper
¼ cup vegetable oil
1½ pounds venison sirloin,
trimmed and shaped like
an elongated loaf of bread
8 juniper berries
2 tablespoons all-purpose flour
1 large egg, beaten
2 ounces sesame seeds

Sauce

1. Make the demi-glace sauce on the previous day, using venison bones instead of veal (see page 182.).

2. Just before serving, combine the demi-glace and wine and bring to boil. Cook until the sauce thickens and season to taste with salt, if desired.

Potatoes

Slice the potatoes into ⅛-inch-thick slices. Melt the butter in a frying pan over medium-high heat. Add half the potatoes, half the thyme and salt to taste. Stir well and then add the remaining potatoes, the cream, remaining thyme and more salt, if desired. Transfer to a roasting pan and bake in a preheated 300 °F oven for 1 hour.

Veal Tenderloin and Venison Sirloin

1. Lightly sprinkle the veal with salt and pepper. Heat 1 tablespoon of oil in a frying pan and sauté the tenderloin for about 4 minutes until lightly browned, turn-

ing constantly. Transfer to a roasting pan and roast in a preheated 325 °F oven for 12 minutes. Cool to room temperature and then transfer the tenderloin to the freezer for 20 minutes.

2. Using a thin-bladed knife, make a "tunnel" in the center of the venison sirloin, twisting the knife as you work to make a cavity large enough to hold the veal tenderloin. Season the sirloin with juniper berries and salt and pepper.

3. When the veal tenderloin is a bit firm from freezing, smear it with oil and stuff it into the tunnel, working it all the way into the cavity.

4. Heat 2 tablespoons of oil in a frying pan over medium-high heat. Cook the stuffed venison for about 4 minutes, turning constantly. Wipe it with paper towels to remove the fat.

5. Roll the stuffed venison in the flour and then brush it with the beaten egg.

6. Spread the sesame seeds in a dry frying pan and toast over high heat for 2 minutes, shaking the pan, until fragrant. Add the meat, turning it to coat it with sesame seeds. Transfer to a roasting pan and bake in a preheated 300 °F oven for 30 to 40 minutes, depending on the thickness of the meat. The venison should be pink inside when done.

Divide the potatoes among 4 warm plates, add braised vegetables if wished.

To Serve

Slice the venison into eight 1-inch slices. Spoon some sauce on each plate and top with 2 pieces of stuffed venison. Position the venison slices in the shape of a butterfly.

Desserts

The Classic
Gundel Crêpe*

4 servings (8 crêpes)

Crêpes

2 large eggs, 1 cup milk
2 drops pure vanilla extract
½ teaspoon granulated sugar
Pinch of salt, Grated zest of 1 lemon
1 cup all-purpose flour
⅓ cup seltzer water, ½ cup vegetable oil

Nut Filling

½ cup heavy cream, ¼ cup granulated sugar

* Klasszikus Gundel-palacsinta

¼ cup light rum
4 ounces ground walnuts
4 ounces finely chopped walnuts
2 ounces raisins
1 heaped tablespoon grated orange zest
1 teaspoon ground cinnamon

Chocolate Sauce

4 ounces semisweet chocolate,
coarsely chopped
1 scant cup milk, 3 large egg yolks
2 tablespoons granulated sugar
2 tablespoons unsweetened cocoa powder
1 tablespoon unsalted butter, melted
2 tablespoons light rum

To Serve

2 tablespoons unsalted butter
Confectioners' sugar

Crêpes

1. In a 2-quart bowl, mix the eggs, milk, vanilla, sugar, lemon zest and salt. Add the flour and stir until smooth. Add the seltzer, a little at a time, until the batter is the consistency of thin sour cream. Set aside to rest for 30 minutes, or cover and refrigerate for at least 2 hours.

2. Brush an 8-inch crêpe or frying pan with oil and heat over medium-high heat. Pour about ⅓ cup of batter into the pan and tilt the pan to cover it with batter. Cook for 20 seconds, turn the crêpe over and cook for 20 seconds longer until set. Put the crêpe on a plate. Make 7 more crêpes with the remaining batter for a total of 8, stacking them on top of each other as they are made.

Nut Filling

1. In a small saucepan, bring the cream and sugar to a boil. Stir in the rum, walnuts, raisins, orange zest and cinnamon and return to the boil. Reduce the heat and cook for 2 or 3 minutes, stirring continuously, until blended. If mixture is very thick, add more cream.

2. Divide the filling among the crêpes and roll into flattened cylinders.

Chocolate Sauce

In a small saucepan, combine the chocolate and milk and heat over low heat, stirring, until the chocolate melts. Remove from the heat and whisk the egg yolks into the chocolate, whisking rapidly to prevent the yolks from cooking. Add the sugar, cocoa, butter and rum and stir until smooth. If the sauce is too thick, add a little more milk.

To Serve

1. Melt the butter in a large frying pan over medium heat. Put 4 of the rolled crêpes in the pan and cook until lightly browned on all sides. Transfer to a warm plate and cover to keep warm. Cook the remaining 4 crêpes in the same way.

2. Place the 2 crêpes on each of 4 warm plates. Pour the sauce over half of each and sprinkle the other half with confectioners' sugar.

If you want to serve the crêpes flaming, fold them into triangle shapes and brown both sides. Put two triangles on each plate, pour chocolate sauce on half of each and sprinkle the other with confectioners' sugar. Heat 6 tablespoons of rum until hot, splatter it over the crêpes and carefully ignite.

According to Imre Gundel, Károly Gundel's son, the classic Gundel crêpe is always served without flaming. Károly Gundel used to heat the crêpes in the oven for a few minutes before serving them.

Our Gundel dessert menu reads: "Flamed on request". Interestingly, this is the only Gundel specialty that is, on occasion, served at New York's Café des Artistes. Until now, the original Gundel Crêpe recipe was known only to five people, and you can be certain that they didn't fly on the same plane! The above is the first time that the authentic recipe is revealed to the crêpe-loving world.

Pancake Tower*

16 servings

4 ounces hazelnuts, coarsely chopped
4 ounces walnuts, coarsely chopped
4 ounces almonds, coarsely chopped
1 cup plus 2 tablespoons unsalted butter, softened
4 ounces raisins, rinsed, ¼ cup rum
½ cup plus 1 teaspoon granulated sugar
Grated zest of 2 lemons, 4 drops pure vanilla extract
10 large eggs, separated, 1¼ cups sour cream
2¼ cups all-purpose flour
⅓ cup vegetable oil, 4 ounces peach jam

* Palacsintatorony

4 ounces blueberry jam
4 ounces strawberry jam, 4 ounces plum jam
4 ounces orange marmalade, Confectioners' sugar

1. Melt ¼ cup of the butter in a 10-inch frying pan. Add the nuts and sauté, stirring constantly, until lightly browned.

2. In a small bowl, combine the raisins and rum and set aside to give the raisins time to plump.

3. Mix the ½ cup of butter, 1 tablespoon of sugar, the lemon zest, and the vanilla extract and stir until smooth. Add the egg yolks, one at a time, and stir until foamy. Be sure one yolk is mixed before adding the next. Fold in the sour cream.

4. Beat the egg whites with the remaining sugar until stiff peaks form. Fold the meringue into the egg yolk foam. Add the flour, stirring constantly.

5. Preheat the oven to 350 °F. Set a pan of hot water on the bottom of the oven. Oil a small roasting pan and put a tablespoon of the remaining butter into the pan. Put the pan in the oven until the butter melts. Meanwhile, heat an oiled 7- or 8-inch crêpe or frying pan over high heat. Spoon about a sixth of the batter into the pan and cook the crêpe over medium heat for 1 minute. Transfer the crêpe to the roasting pan, browned side up. Bake for about 8 minutes until puffed and lightly browned. Remove from the pan with a spatula and set aside, covered, to keep warm. Continue baking pancakes with the remaining batter to make a total of 6 pancakes. Add butter to the pan and more water before baking each pancake.

6. Spread one kind of jam on 1 pancake, top with a few nuts and drained, plumped raisins. Top with another pancake and spread with another flavor of jam and top with nuts and raisins. Continue until all the pancakes, jam, nuts and raisins are used. Top with the sixth pancake.

7. Sprinkle the top of the pancake tower with confectioners' sugar and slice before serving.

Crêpe Soufflé with Sour Cherries[*]

10 servings

Filling

1 quart canned sour cherry compote
2 ounces cornstarch
7 tablespoons granulated sugar, Juice of 1 lemon
Grated zest of 1 lemon, 2 tablespoons unsalted butter
½ cup heavy cream, 4 large egg yolks
2 drops pure vanilla extract

Sauce

3 cups milk, ¾ cup granulated sugar
4 drops pure vanilla extract
Finely grated zest of 1 lemon
6 large egg yolks, lightly beaten
1 tablespoon all-purpose flour

Filling

1. In a large saucepan, combine the compote, cornstarch, 5 tablespoons of sugar, lemon juice, lemon zest and 1 cup of water, bring to a boil over high heat and cook for about 30 seconds, stirring. Remove from the heat and add the vanilla extract. Stir to mix and then set aside to cool to lukewarm.

2. Rub the butter in the bottom and up the sides of a loaf pan and line it with 5 or 6 crêpes, arranging them

* Meggyes palacsintafelfújt

so that they overhang the sides and can be folded back over the top to cover a filling.

3. Lay the remaining crêpes on a work surface and spread the compote filling on them. Roll them into slightly flattened cylinders. Lay the rolled crepes in the loaf pan, stacking them if necessary.

4. In a small bowl, combine the cream, egg yolks, the remaining 2 tablespoons of sugar and vanilla extract and whisk until smooth. Pour over the rolled crêpes and gently shake the pan to distribute the sauce evenly. Fold the overhanging crêpes over the rolled crêpes and wrap the entire pan with foil. Set the pan in roasting pan and add enough hot water to come about a third of the way up the sides of the pan. Bake in a preheated 300 °F oven for about 1½ hours, adding more very hot water to the larger pan, if necessary. Remove from the oven and let the pan cool in the larger pan and water for about 1 hour.

Sauce

1. In a saucepan, combine the milk, sugar, vanilla extract and lemon zest and bring to a boil over medium-high heat, stirring. Whisk the egg yolks and flour in the top of double boiler (the pan should not be set over heat). Remove 1 cup of the hot milk from the pan and whisk into the egg yolks and flour. Whisk constantly to prevent the egg yolks from cooking. Pour in the remaining hot milk and set the top of the double boiler over boiling water. Cook, stirring, for about 5 minutes until thickened and smooth.

2. Unwrap the loaf pan and invert the crêpe loaf onto a platter or cutting board. Using a long-bladed knife that has been dipped in cold water and wiped dry between every cut, slice the crêpe loaf into slices. Serve with the sauce.

Strawberry Strudel Cake*

4 servings

Dough

8 sheets phyllo dough
3 tablespoons vegetable oil

Strawberry Cream

10 ounces fresh strawberries,
hulled and coarsely chopped
½ cup confectioners' sugar
2 large egg yolks
1 teaspoon unflavored gelatin
2 teaspoons cornstarch

* Epres rétestortácska

2 tablespoons
strawberry-flavored liqueur
2 cups whipping cream,
whipped until stiff and chilled

Vanilla Sauce

¾ cup milk
2 tablespoons plus 1 teaspoon sugar
2 large egg yolks
2 tablespoons all-purpose flour
4 drops pure vanilla extract

Strawberry Sauce

8 ounces fresh strawberries,
hulled and coarsely chopped
½ cup confectioners' sugar
1½ tablespoons strawberry-flavored liqueur

Garnish

4 large fresh whole strawberries
4 sprigs fresh mint

Dough

Lay 2 sheets of phyllo dough on a work surface and brush 1 with oil. Lay the other on top of the first and brush it with oil. Using a 2-inch cookie or biscuit cutter, cut out 6 disks and transfer to an oiled baking sheet or pan. Bake in a preheated 350 °F oven for 6 or 7 minutes until browned. Remove from the baking sheet and set aside on wire racks to cool. Repeat with the remaining sheet of phyllo dough and oil to make 24 disks. (It's a good idea to make a few extra disks, in case any break.)

Strawberry Cream

1. Put the strawberries and 2 tablespoons of confectioners' sugar in the top of a double boiler or a metal bowl and crush with the back of a spoon or fork. Set over about an inch of boiling water and cook, whisking, until the sugar melts and the mixture is relatively smooth. Transfer to another bowl to cool slightly.

2. In the top of a double boiler, combine the egg yolks, gelatin, cornstarch and remaining confectioners' sugar and set over about an inch of boiling water, stirring constantly for 5 or 6 minutes until smooth. Remove from the heat and gently stir in the liqueur.

3. Fold the egg mixture into the strawberry-sugar mixture. Fold in the chilled whipped cream. Cover and refrigerate.

Vanilla Sauce

In the top of a double boiler or a metal bowl, whisk together the milk, sugar, egg yolks, flour and vanilla extract. Set over about an inch of boiling water and cook, whisking constantly, for 5 or 6 minutes until smooth. Remove from the heat and let cool.

Strawberry Sauce

In a metal bowl, combine the strawberries and sugar and crush with the back of a spoon. Push the mixture through a strainer and flavor with the liqueur.

To Serve

Separate the disks into 4 groups of 6 each. Spread the strawberry cream between the disks, stacking them on top of each other to make 4 stacks. Do not spread cream on the top disk. Pool the vanilla sauce on each of 4 plates and drizzle with the strawberry sauce. Set a filled stack on the sauce and sprinkle with confectioners' sugar. Garnish with whole strawberries and mint sprigs.

Cottage Cheese Dumplings Wampetich Style[*]

4 servings

2 cups cottage cheese, drained in a sieve
3 large egg yolks
Grated zest of 1 lemon
1 cup plus 2 tablespoons semolina flour
½ teaspoon salt
⅓ cup vegetable oil
2 cups chopped strawberries,
peaches or seedless green or red grapes
(about 10 ounces)
1¼ cups chopped walnuts (about 5 ounces)
1 cup confectioners' sugar
1 cup sour cream

* Túrógombóc Wampetich módra

1. Put the cottage cheese, egg yolks, zest and flour in a large bowl and stir to mix. Cover and refrigerate for 30 minutes until firm.

2. Bring 2 quarts of water to a boil. Add the oil and salt and return to the boil. Gather about ¼ cup of the batter between dampened palms, press some fruit into the center and form the batter into a dumpling enclosing the fruit. Make more dumplings with the remaining batter to make 12 dumplings. Gently drop the dumplings into the boiling water and cook until they rise to the surface. You may do this in batches.

3. Using a skimmer or large slotted spoon, lift the dumplings from the water and drain. Roll the hot dumplings in the nuts, place 3 on each plate and sprinkle with confectioners' sugar. Serve immediately with a generous dollop of sour cream.

This was a popular dessert at the Wampetich restaurant, which was Gundel's predecessor in City Park. It also has been a great favorite in Hungarian households for the last 150 years. I discovered an old recipe for the dumplings in an old notebook and have rewritten it for Gundel.

Rigó Jancsi with His Own "Stradivari"*

16 servings

Sponge Cake
3 large eggs, separated
½ cup granulated sugar
½ cup all-purpose flour
2 tablespoons unsweetened cocoa powder

Cream
8 ounces milk chocolate, coarsely chopped
2 pints whipping cream, whipped to firm peaks

Glaze
3 ounces milk chocolate, coarsely chopped
1 tablespoon vegetable oil

* Rigó Jancsi „Stradivarijával"

Sponge Cake

1. In a 2-quart bowl, combine the egg yolks and ¼ cup of the sugar. Whisk for about 10 minutes until foamy and set aside. Combine the remaining ¼ cup of sugar with the egg whites and beat to stiff peaks. Fold the whites into the yolk foam. Whisk the flour and cocoa together and then gently fold the dry ingredients into the batter.

2. Line a baking sheet with waxed paper and sprinkle it with flour. Spread the batter over the wax paper, using a kitchen knife to spread it into a layer about 16 inches long and nearly as wide as the baking sheet. Bake in a preheated 350 °F over for 8 to 10 minutes until the cake springs back when lightly pressed in the center. Invert onto a large metal rack and let cool for about 5 minutes. Peel the wax paper from the cake and let cool completely.

Cream

1. In the top of a double boiler or a metal bowl set over simmering water, melt the chocolate, stirring until smooth. Remove from the heat and stir in a third of the whipped cream. When incorporated, add the remaining whipped cream and stir gently and carefully. Do not over mix.

2. Using a long serrated knife, cut the cake horizontally into 2 thin layers. Transfer 1 layer to a flat platter or tray, cut side up, and spread the chocolate cream over it. Work quickly as the cream collapses easily. Refrigerate until firm. Put the second layer on a flat tray or work surface, cut side down, and set aside.

Glaze

In the top of a double boiler or a metal bowl set over simmering water, combine the chocolate and oil and heat, stirring constantly, until the chocolate melts and is smooth. Pour the glaze over the second cake layer, spreading it with a dry knife to cover the cake evenly. When the glaze firms up, remove the chilled layer from the refrigerator and carefully set the glazed layer on top of it.

To Serve

Cut the cake into 2-inch squares, using a thin-bladed knife dipped in warm water and wiped dry between each cut.

This popular dessert has a romantic history: Pákozdi Rigó Jancsi, the famous gypsy musician, was performing in the Alhambra in Paris when Belgium's Count Chimay and his wife were in the audience. The lady, who came from a wealthy American family, fell in love with the handsome gypsy musician, left her husband, and traveled to Hungary with Rigó Jancsi. A Hungarian confectioner created this rich cake and, because he had a good sense of public relations, named it after Rigó Jancsi. Although the confectioner's name was forgotten long ago, the romantic story behind the cake remains. At Gundel, when we serve the cake, Gundel's famed gypsy band plays in the background.

Dove in a Cage[*]

4 servings

Coffee Bavarois

4 ounces white chocolate, coarsely chopped
¼ cup heavy cream
2 tablespoons brewed coffee
¼ teaspoon unflavored gelatin
2 cups whipping cream, whipped to stiff peaks
1 tablespoon vegetable oil

Vanilla Sauce

1 cup milk, ¼ cup granulated sugar
1 vanilla bean, 3 large egg yolks

[*] Galamb a kalitkában

Dove

2 ounces marzipan

Caramel Cage

4 ounces sugar cubes
½ teaspoon white wine vinegar
¼ cup chocolate sauce

Coffee Bavarois

1. In the top of a double boiler or in a metal bowl set over simmering water, melt the chocolate, stirring until smooth. Remove from the heat but leave the top of the double boiler set over the hot water to keep it warm.

2. In a saucepan, bring the cream to a boil over medium-high heat. Remove from the heat and stir in the coffee. Pour the cream into the melted chocolate and whisk until smooth. Set aside to cool to room temperature.

3. Mix the gelatin with 1 teaspoon of water and heat in a small metal bowl set over boiling water, stirring until the gelatin melts.

4. Fold the whipped cream into the cooled chocolate-cream mixture. Add the hot gelatin mixture and stir until smooth.

5. Oil 4 small 2-inch-diameter cake pans, each 2 inches high. Dust with confectioners' sugar.

6. Cover a baking sheet with wax paper and set the cake pans on the baking sheet. Fill each with coffee bavarois and freeze for about 30 minutes until firm. When frozen, transfer the bavarois to the refrigerator.

Vanilla Sauce

1. In a saucepan, combine the milk and 2 tablespoons

of sugar. Split the vanilla bean in half and scrape the seeds into the milk. Reserve the bean for another use.

2. Whisk the eggs yolks in a mixing bowl. Add the remaining 2 tablespoons of sugar and whisk until smooth.

3. Bring the milk mixture to a boil. Immediately remove from the heat and pour half of the hot milk into the egg yolks, whisking constantly to temper the eggs. Pour the egg mixture into the milk remaining in the saucepan and set over medium-low heat, whisking to mix. Switch to a wooden spoon and gently stir the sauce, scraping along the bottom of the pan. Cook for about 45 seconds until the milk begins to steam. Do not let the milk boil. The sauce should be thick enough to coat the back of the spoon. Remove from the heat and set aside for 5 to 10 minutes, stirring occasionally, to cool slightly. (The sauce can be covered and refrigerated for up to 2 days. Reheat gently before serving or serve cool.)

Doves

Shape 4 white doves from the marzipan.

Caramel Cages

1. Fill a heavy 1-quart pot halfway with water and bring to a boil. Discard the hot water.

2. Put the sugar cubes, 2 tablespoons of water and ¼ teaspoon of vinegar in the clean, warm pot and bring to a boil over medium heat. Boil without stirring until the sugar bubbles and turns golden yellow.

3. Wrap a cup-sized soup ladle with aluminum foil and rub the foil with oil. Take a tablespoonful of melted sugar and drizzle it slowly in the cup of the ladle, making a net-like pattern. (If the sugar hardens in the pot, set it over the heat and melt carefully to avoid burning.)

Lay the ladle aside for about 3 minutes to let the sugar harden. Carefully remove the foil from the ladle and then slip the foil from the sugar to reveal a sugar cage. Set aside in a cool, dry place. Repeat to make 4 cages.

To Serve

Pool the vanilla sauce on each of 4 plates. Pour a thin circle of chocolate sauce around it. Unmold the bavarois and set 1 on top of the sauce. Put the doves on top of the bavarois. Invert a caramel cage over each. Serve immediately.

A topnotch pastry chef in Hungary must combine the skill of his profession with the techniques of a sculptor and the lyricism of a poet. This captivating dessert is a good example of this holy trinity. Even if you don't plan to make it, you might find it interesting to learn about the process.

In Hungary, it is common practice to bury a split vanilla bean in a tightly lidded jar filled with granulated sugar. The bean infuses the sugar, which is then used to flavor desserts instead of vanilla extract.

Dobos Torte[*]

16 slices

Sponge Cake leaves

8 large eggs, separated
1½ cup sugar
2 cups flour
1 tablespoon vegetable oil

Filling

4 large eggs
1½ cups plus 1 teaspoon sugar
2 teaspoons vanilla extract
1 tablespoon all-purpose flour
9 ounces milk chocolate, coarsely chopped
1 cup unsalted butter, softened

"Dobos" Sugar Crust

1¼ cups granulated sugar

Sponge Cake Leaves

1. Beat the egg yolks with half of the sugar until foamy and lemon colored. Whip the egg whites with the remaining sugar until they form stiff peaks. Gently fold the egg yolks into the beaten whites. Stirring the batter

* Dobostorta

with a wooden spoon, add the flour by sprinkling it over the top of the batter and gently mixing it in, taking care not to deflate the foam.

2. Lightly oil a baking sheet and dust it with flour. Trace the outline of a 10-inch diameter cake pan. Pour a sixth of the batter in the center of the marked circle and using a kitchen knife, spread it out to fill the circle evenly. The batter will be very thin. Bake in a preheated 350 °F oven for 8 to 10 minutes or until golden and the center of the cake springs back when gently pressed. Lift the cake layer from the baking sheet with a pancake turner or spatula and set aside on a wire rack to cool. Repeat to make 6 layers. When cool, trim the layers so that they are even and the same size.

Filling

1. In the top of double boiler or metal bowl, beat the eggs, sugar and vanilla until smooth. Set over about an inch of boiling water and heat, whisking, until a little warmer than lukewarm (about 115 °F). Remove from the heat, stir in the flour and whisk until foamy. Set aside.

2. In the top of a double boiler or in a metal bowl set over simmering water, melt the chocolate, stirring until smooth but not hot.

3. Whisk the butter into the chocolate. Add the egg foam and stir just until combined. Set aside 1 cup of the filling. Spread the remaining filling on 5 of the cake layers, reserving the most attractive layer for the top of the cake. Stack the filled layers and then frost the sides of the cake. Refrigerate for 1 or 2 hours until the filling is firm.

"Dobos" Sugar Crust

Put the sugar in a heavy ½-quart saucepan and heat over high heat without stirring until golden brown. Set the reserved cake layer on a rack set in a pan and pour the caramel over it, smoothing it with a table knife. Rub butter on a long, thin-bladed knife and trace 16 wedges in the caramel. When traced, cut about halfway through the cake layer. Work quickly as the caramel will cool and crack. Set the top layer on top of the filled cake. When the caramel is completely cool, cut the cake into 16 slices.

Joseph C. Dobos, born in 1847, had a fabulous specialty food shop in Budapest, where he stocked more than 60 different cheeses and 22 Champagnes. He managed to import every rare seasonal delicacy imaginable. It was in this shop that he created and sold his famous Dobos torte in 1887–and where he devised packaging so he could ship the cake to foreign countries. The sensation of the Millennary Exposition in 1896 was the Dobos Pavilion, where the Dobos Torte was served. Soon poor imitations of the cake began appearing everywhere. This prompted Dobos to publish the authentic recipe in 1906 and donate it to the Budapest Pastry and Gingerbread Makers Guild.

Ilona Torte[*]

12 slices

Torte

5 ounces semisweet chocolate, coarsely chopped
1 cup sugar, 6 tablespoons unsalted butter
8 large eggs, separated
8 ounces walnuts, ground
2 tablespoons white bread crumbs
Pinch of salt

Filling

3 tablespoons espresso powder
8 ounces semisweet chocolate, coarsely chopped
3 large egg yolks, 1 cup granulated sugar
1¼ cups unsalted butter, cut into pieces and chilled

Garnish

2 tablespoons chopped walnuts

Torte

1. In the top of a double boiler or in a metal bowl set over simmering water, combine the chocolate, water and cook for 5 or 6 minutes, stirring, until smooth.

2. In a bowl, whisk the butter and egg yolks until light and foamy. Add the chocolate, ground walnuts and bread crumbs.

3. In another bowl, combine the egg whites, salt and 1 teaspoon of ice water and beat to stiff peaks. Gently

* Ilona torta

fold the whites into the chocolate mixture. Scrape the batter into a lightly oiled and floured 10-inch cake pan that is 3 inches deep. Bake in a preheated 375 °F oven for 20 to 25 minutes until a toothpick inserted in the center comes out clean. Cool the cake on a wire rack.

Filling

1. In a small cup, stir the espresso powder with 1 table-spoon of boiling water. In the top of a double boiler or in a metal bowl set over simmering water, combine the chocolate and espresso and heat, stirring, until the chocolate melts and the mixture is smooth. Set aside to cool completely.

2. Put the egg yolks and sugar in a metal mixing bowl or the top of a double boiler and set it over an inch or so of simmering water (the bowl should not touch the water). Whisk until the sugar dissolves and the yolks feel warm. Remove the bowl from the heat. Using an electric mixer set on high speed, whip the whites until stiff peaks form. Reduce the speed to medium and beat until the meringue cools to room temperature. Start adding the butter, a piece at a time, not adding the next piece until the previous one is incorporated. When all the butter is added, increase the speed to high and beat until smooth.

3. With the mixer on medium speed, add the cooled chocolate mixture and beat until mixed Increase the speed to high and beat briefly.

To Serve

Slice the cake into 2 layers. Fill them with about half of the filling and use the remaining to frost the top and sides of the cake. Decorate with the chopped walnuts. Refrigerate for 2 hours until chilled. Serve chilled.

Baked Cheesecake with Hot Fruits*

12 servings

Cake

¼ cup unsalted butter, chilled and cubed
¾ cup confectioners' sugar
1 large egg, 2¼ cups all-purpose flour
½ cup walnuts, chopped, ½ cup sliced almonds
¼ cup unsalted butter, softened, ½ cup light brown sugar

Cream Cheese

1¼ pounds cream cheese, ¼ cup corn starch
1¼ cups sour cream
2 tablespoons Amaretto liqueur
1 cup plus 1 teaspoon granulated sugar
Grated zest of 2 lemons, 3 large eggs

* Sült sajttorta forró gyümölcsökkel

Fruit Ragout

¼ cup unsalted butter, ½ cup sugar
2 cups semisweet white wine
1 large firm apple, peeled, cored and cut into cubes
1 orange, peeled and segmented
1 cup canned sour cherry compote

Cake

1. Sprinkle the chilled butter over the confectioners' sugar and using your fingers, a fork or pastry blender combine until the mixture resembles crumbs. Work quickly to prevent the butter from melting. Add the egg and flour and knead until the dough is crumbly. Press the dough into a 10-inch cake pan and bake in a pre-heated 350 °F oven for 3 or 4 minutes. During baking, break the dough into pieces with a wooden spoon. Remove the pan from the oven and set on a wire rack to cool. Invert the crumbled cake onto a work surface and break into smaller crumbs with a rolling pin.

2. Spread the walnuts and almonds on a baking sheet and roast in a preheated 350 °F oven for about 5 minutes, shaking the pan several times, until lightly browned and fragrant. In a large saucepan, combine the softened butter, cake crumbs and brown sugar and stir until well mixed. Stir in the nuts.

3. Line a 10-inch round cake pan with foil so that the foil overhangs the sides of the pan. Set the pan on a baking sheet. Press the nut dough over the bottom of the pan to make a thick bottom crust.

Cream Cheese

In a large bowl, combine the cream cheese, sour cream, sugar, eggs, liqueur, vanilla and lemon zest and beat until foamy and smooth. Pour over dough and bake in a preheated 300 °F oven for 2½ hours until the cheese filling is set. Open the oven door a few times to release any built-up steam. Let the cake cool in a turned-off oven with the door propped open for about 1 hour. Cool further, still in the pan, on a wire rack.

Fruit Ragout

Melt the butter in a 10-inch frying pan until golden brown. Add the sugar and wine, bring to a boil and cook until the sugar dissolves. Add the apple, orange and compote to the pan and bring the mixture to a boil, tossing to coat the fruit with butter and sugar. Serve hot.

To Serve

Lift the cake from the pan, using the foil as guides. Slice the cake using a long-bladed knife dipped in warm water and wiped dry between every slice. Serve at room temperature or reheat the slices gently in a 200 °F oven (as we do at Gundel). Serve the hot fruit next to each slice of cheesecake (see photo).

Select fruit for the ragout according to the season. The cake will be easier to cut if you make it the day before and refrigerate it until serving. If you prefer, warm it in a low oven until warm but not hot. You could bake the cake in a springform pan and release the sides of the pan when the cake is completely cool. If so, there is not need to line the pan with foil.

Sauces and Side Dishes

Our Vinaigrette Dressing*

4 servings

2 tablespoons honey
½ cup white wine vinegar
2 tablespoons olive oil
Salt and freshly ground white pepper
3 tablespoons chopped fresh parsley
2 tablespoons finely chopped fresh tarragon leaves
2 tablespoons capers, drained and chopped
2 tablespoons chopped leek
5 tablespoons grated cornichons

Bring to honey to a boil in a small saucepan, remove from the heat and stir in vinegar and olive oil and season to taste with salt and pepper. Add the parsley, tarragon, capers, leeks and cornichons and stir well. Set aside to cool and serve in a sauce boat.
This is a good dressing for asparagus or fish.

Gribiche Sauce**

4 servings

2 hardcooked large eggs
1 cup crushed ice

* Vinaigrette-mártás
** Gribiche mártás

1 teaspoon Dijon-style mustard
Salt and freshly ground white pepper
½ cup olive oil
1 tablespoon white wine vinegar
1 tablespoon chopped cornichons
1 tablespoons capers,
drained and chopped
1 tablespoon chopped leek
1 tablespoon chopped
fresh parsley
1 tablespoon chopped fresh
tarragon leaves

1. Halve the eggs and remove the yolks. Put the yolks in a small bowl and mash with a fork. Cut the whites into thin strips and set aside.

2. Put the crushed ice in a 2-quart bowl pot and set the small bowl with the egg yolks on the ice. Add the mustard and season to taste with salt and pepper. Whisk to mix and then, still whisking, add the olive oil in a slow, steady stream until incorporated and the consistency of mayonnaise. Whisk in the vinegar and then stir in the cornichons, capers, leek, parsley and tarlragon. Gently stir in the egg whites.

Piquant Sage Dressing*

4 servings

2 large egg yolks
2 tablespoons mustard
1 cup vegetable oil, refrigerated for 1 hour
4 tablespoons chopped fresh parsley
4 tablespoons chopped fresh sage
½ cup olive oil
Salt and freshly ground white pepper
Juice of 1 lemon
½ cup plain yogurt

1. In a small bowl, stir together the egg yolks and mustard until well blended. Slowly add the chilled oil, whisking constantly, until the mixture is the consistency of mayonnaise.

2. In a blender or food processor, puree the parsley, sage and olive oil. Stir into the mayonnaise. Season to taste with salt and pepper. Stir in the lemon juice and then whisk in the yogurt.

Serve with cold fish dishes, vegetables, stuffed eggs, etc.

* Hideg zsályamártás

Fish Stock*

Makes about 1 cup

2 pounds fish bones and head(s)
4 black peppercorns
¼ lemon

1. Put the fish bones, head, peppercorns, lemon and 1 quart of water in a 1-gallon pot. Bring to a boil over medium heat, reduce the heat and simmer for about 1½ hours until reduced to one quarter. Skim any foam that rises to the surface during cooking.

2. Strain the stock through a cheesecloth-lined sieve into a bowl. Cool slightly, cover and refrigerate until ready to use.

Veal Stock**

Makes about 1 quart

¼ cup vegetable oil
4 pounds veal bones,
sawed or chopped into 4 inch pieces
Greens from 1 stalk celery
1 sprig parsley

* Hal alaplé
** Barna borjúalaplé

1 bay leaf
½ teaspoon crushed
black peppercorns
1 teaspoon granulated sugar
1 onion, chopped
1 stalk celery, diced
1 carrot, peeled and diced
1 parsnip, peeled and diced
1 tablespoon tomato puree

1. In a 2-gallon stockpot, heat 3 tablespoons of the oil over medium-high heat and brown the bones until lightly browned, stirring continuously. (Or roast the bones in a preheated 400 °F oven without oil.) Pour off fat and let the bones cool.

2. Pour 1 gallon of cold water over the bones. Bring to a boil over high heat, reduce the heat to low and simmer for about 3 hours, skimming any foam that rises to the surface from time to time. Stir in celery greens, parsley, bay leaf and peppercorns.

3. In a 10-inch frying pan, cook the sugar, stirring, until lightly browned. Add the remaining 1 tablespoon of oil, the onion, celery, carrot and parsnip and sauté for a few minutes until the vegetables begin to caramelize. Add the tomato puree and sauté, stirring continuously, until blended. Pour ½ cup of water over the vegetables and then stir this mixture into to the stockpot with the bones. Simmer, partially covered, for 1 hour, skimming the surface frequently.

4. Strain the stock through a cheesecloth-lined sieve into a bowl. Cool slightly, cover and refrigerate until cold. Remove the hardened fat from the surface. Refrigerate until ready to use.

Brown Sauce*

Makes about 3 cups

1 tablespoon vegetable oil
1 onion, chopped
1 small carrot, peeled and diced
1 small parsnip, peeled and diced
1 small celery stalk, diced
1 teaspoon tomato puree
1 quart Veal Stock (see page 179.)
2 tablespoons all-purpose flour

1. In a large stockpot, heat the oil over medium-high heat. Add the onion, carrot, parsnip and celery and sauté until golden brown. Add the tomato puree and sauté for 2 or 3 minutes longer. Add the Veal Stock.

2. In a dry 6-inch frying pan, sauté the flour over medium heat, stirring with a wooden spoon just until lightly browned. Remove from heat and continue stirring to prevent the flour from burning in the still-hot pan. Set aside to cool. Add the flour slowly to the stockpot, whisking continuously until smooth. Simmer for about 1 hour. Strain the sauce through a fine sieve. Transfer the vegetables to a bowl containing ⅓ cup of water and then stir the vegetables and water into the sauce. Reheat gently for serving.

* Barna alapmártás

Glace de Viande*
(Glace de Viande)

Makes about 1 cup

1 quart Veal Stock (see page 179.)

1. Boil the veal stock in a heavy saucepan until reduce by half, continually skimming the fat from the surface ofthe stock.

2. Pour into a smaller, clean saucepan. Bring to a boil and cook until reduced by half and thickened. Use immediately or refrigerate.

We recommend this in preparing or enriching sauces. You will need no more than half a teaspoon or so to bring alive soups and sauces. If refrigerated, the glaze will gel and will keep well for a week. If you want to keep it longer, cut the jelly into small cubes, wrap in foil and freeze.

Demi-Glace Sauce**

Makes about 3 cups

3 cups Veal Stock (see page 179.)
3 cups Brown Sauce (see page 181.)
2 tablespoons Glace de Viande (see page 182.)

1. In a large stockpot, bring the stock to a boil. Reduce the heat and simmer until reduced to a third. Add the brown sauce and simmer for 30 minutes longer.

* Glace de viande *(húskivonat-húsfény)*
** Demi-glace mártás

2. Stir in the Glace de Viande and simmer for just a few minutes longer until heated through and blended. Strain through a cheesecloth-lined sieve into a bowl. Use immediately or cool slightly, cover and refrigerate until ready to use.

This is the basis for many different sauces, which are finished with the addition of wine, seasonings, cream or a combination.

Wild Mushroom Sauce with Red Wine*

4 servings

½ cup dry red wine, such as Egri Merlot
1 tablespoon finely chopped onion
2 tablespoons unsalted butter
8 ounces mixed sliced mushrooms,
such as portobello, cepes,
shiitake and chanterelles
Salt and freshly ground white pepper
1 cup Demi-Glace Sauce (see page 182.)

In a saucepan, combine the wine and onion and bring to a boil over high heat. Reduce the heat and simmer until reduced by three-quarters. Add the butter and mushrooms and simmer, stirring, for 2 or 3 minutes. Season with salt and pepper. Stir in the Demi-Glace Sauce, bring to a simmer and cook for 4 or 5 minutes. Serve immediately.

* Vörösboros vadgombamártás

183

Maltaise Sauce*

4 servings

½ cup dry white wine
Grated zest of 1 blood orange
7 tablespoons clarified butter, melted
4 large egg yolks
¼ cup fresh blood orange juice,
or another juice orange
Salt

1. In a saucepan, combine the wine and zest, bring to a boil and cook for 2 or 3 minutes. Strain the zest from the wine and reserve.

2. In the top of a double boil or a metal bowl, combine the egg yolks, orange juice and a pinch of salt and stir to mix. Set over boiling water and cook stirring continuously, until blended. Add the wine and then slowly add the melted butter, stirring continuously. Remove from the heat, stir for a few minutes longer, and then stir in the orange zest.

* Máltai mártás

Garlic Compote[*]

4 servings

1 bay leaf, 2 allspice
1 knob fresh ginger,
about the size of a hazelnut, peeled
1 cup peeled garlic cloves
½ cup granulated sugar
2 cups white wine
1 teaspoon cornstarch

1. In a small saucepan, heat ½ cup water over medium heat. Add the bay leaf, allspice and ginger and simmer for 10 minutes until reduced by half.

2. Put the garlic cloves in a strainer and submerge the strainer in a saucepan full of boiling water for 2 minutes.

3. In a 2-quart saucepan, cook the sugar, stirring continuously, for about 3 minutes until golden. Pour in the wine and simmer for about 3 minutes longer until the sugar dissolves.

4. Strain the spiced liquid into the wine, add the scalded garlic and bring to a boil. Reduce the heat and simmer for 15 minutes.

5. In a small cup, stir the cornstarch with 1 tablespoon of water. Pour slowly into the sauce and boil for about 2 minutes. Transfer to a glass jar, cover and refrigerate for a few weeks. Or, pour into sterilized canning jars and seal.

Serve with roasts, especially lamb. This compote is best served at room temperature.

* Fokhagymakompót

Little Pinched Noodles*

Enough for 8 servings of soup

1 cup all-purpose flour
1 large egg, lightly beaten
Salt

1. Sift ⅔ cup of the flour into a bowl. Make a well in the center and crack the egg into it. Sprinkle with salt and knead until a stiff dough forms. Add the remaining flour if the dough is not stiff enough.

2. On a lightly floured work surface, pinch flat, rounded, fingernail-size or smaller bits from the dough, occasionally sprinkling with flour. Cook in 1½ quarts of simmering soup or salted water for 10 to 12 minutes or until the noodles rise to the surface.

3. If cooked in water, drain and rinse with cold water.

For four portions of soup, use only half of the noodles. Dry the rest on a floured board for two days, and then store in a container or plastic bag in a cool, dry place. There are no two cooks who pinch these noodles into identical shapes–all have individual thumbprints, in more ways than one.

* Csipetke

Egg Dumplings[*]

4 servings

4 teaspoons salt
2½ cups all-purpose flour
2 large eggs
1 tablespoon vegetable oil

1. In a large pot, bring 2½ quarts water of water and 3½ teaspoons of salt to a boil over high heat.

2. In a mixing bowl, combine the flour, eggs and the remaining ½ teaspoon of salt with ⅔ cup of water and stir until a dough forms.

3. Divide the dough into quarters and put one quarter on a dampened cutting board, flattening it slightly. With a knife dipped in the boiling salted water, cut a strip from the dough, dip the knife in the water again and then cut the strip into ½-inch-long dumplings. Push the dumplings off the knife blade into the boiling water. Repeat until all the dough is used. Stir the water while dumplings are cooking. When they rise to the surface, drain and rinse with warm water. Toss the dumplings in oil and serve hot.

* Galuska

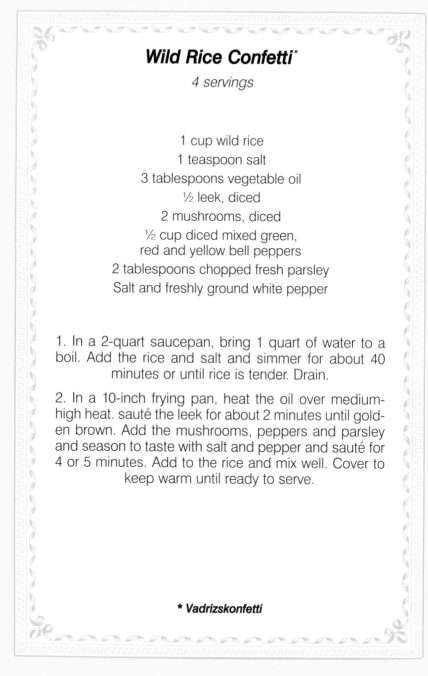

*Wild Rice Confetti**

4 servings

1 cup wild rice
1 teaspoon salt
3 tablespoons vegetable oil
½ leek, diced
2 mushrooms, diced
½ cup diced mixed green,
red and yellow bell peppers
2 tablespoons chopped fresh parsley
Salt and freshly ground white pepper

1. In a 2-quart saucepan, bring 1 quart of water to a boil. Add the rice and salt and simmer for about 40 minutes or until rice is tender. Drain.

2. In a 10-inch frying pan, heat the oil over medium-high heat. sauté the leek for about 2 minutes until golden brown. Add the mushrooms, peppers and parsley and season to taste with salt and pepper and sauté for 4 or 5 minutes. Add to the rice and mix well. Cover to keep warm until ready to serve.

* Vadrizskonfetti

Potato Croquettes*

8 servings

8 medium-sized potatoes, peeled
4 large egg yolks
Grated fresh nutmeg
Salt
Dried white bread crumbs
1 quart vegetable oil

1. Cook the potatoes in salted boiling water for 15 to 20 minutes until tender. Drain and then push the potatoes through a sieve into a large saucepan. Stir or whisk, breaking up the potatoes, until cool. Add the egg yolks, season with nutmeg and salt and mix well.

2. Form the potato dough into 8 balls. Roll in the bread crumbs until coated.

3. In a deep skillet or saucepan, heat the oil over high heat until very hot. Deep fry the croquettes for about 4 minutes until browned. Drain on paper towels.

You can make dried white bread crumbs by grinding toasted white bread in a blender.

* Burgonyakrokett

Mashed Potatoes with Onion*

4 servings

4 medium-sized potatoes, peeled
5 tablespoons vegetable oil
2 onions, finely chopped
Salt and freshly ground white pepper
1 tablespoon dried bread crumbs

1. Cook the potatoes in salted boiling water for 15 to 20 minutes until tender. Drain and let cool for about 5 minutes. Using a potato masher or fork, mash the potatoes (do not puree them).

2. In a frying pan, heat ¼ cup of the oil over medium-high heat. Add the onions and sauté until golden brown. Mix the onions into the potatoes and season to taste with salt and pepper.

3. Heat the remaining tablespoon of oil in a nonstick frying pan over medium heat. Spread the bread crumbs in the pan and spoon the mashed potatoes over them. Press the potatoes into the pan to cover the bread crumbs and cook for 8 minutes without turning. Invert the potato cake onto a plate and then return it to the pan, with the uncooked side down. Cook for about 8 minutes longer until both sides are browned. Cut into 4 slices and serve hot.

* Hagymás törtburgonya

Fried Crisp Onion Rings*

4 servings

4 large onions
½ cup flour
1 quart sunflower oil

1. Cut the onions into paper-thin slices, keeping them in intact rings. Use a slicing machine or a shredder instead of a knife to ensure thin slices.

2. Spread the onion slices on a baking sheet and sprinkle with flour. Toss gently with your hands so that the slices are well coated.

3. In a deep skillet or saucepan, heat the oil over medium-high heat until very hot. Deep fry half the onions, stirring, until golden brown. Remove from the oil and drain on paper towels. Let the oil regain its high heat and deep fry the remaining onions.

* Ropogósra sült hagymakarikák

Index

ISBN 963 9207 83 7

Printed by
Alföldi Nyomda Rt., Debrecen
Responsible manager: Géza György general manager

77 RECIPES

GUNDEL

NEW HUNGARIAN COOKBOOK

77 RECIPES

GUNDEL

NEW HUNGARIAN COOKBOOK